To [illegible]es,
[illegible] wishes,
Jerry De Katz

Liberation Theology

By The Same Authors:

The Believers Handbook

The Deacons Handbook

The Elders Handbook

God's Yardstick

By Lester DeKoster

All Ye That Labor (Eerdmans)

Christian And The John Birch Society (Eerdmans)

Citizen And The John Birch Society (Eerdmans)

Communism And Christian Faith (Eerdmans)

How To Read The Bible (Baker)

Vocabulary Of Communism (Eerdmans)

Work (CLP)

Abridged and Edited:

The Federalist Papers (Eerdmans)

Locke's Second Essay on Civil Government (Eerdmans)

Liberation Theology

The Church's Future Shock

EXPLANATION ANALYSIS CRITIQUE ALTERNATIVE

Gerard Berghoef
Lester DeKoster

Christian's Library Press
Grand Rapids, Michigan 49501

Post Office Box 2226
Grand Rapids, Michigan 49501

ISBN 0-934874-07-7

For Audrey *and* Ruth

Jesus then said to the Jews who had believed in him,
"If you continue in my word,
you are truly my disciples,
and you will know the truth,
and the truth will make you free."

(John 8:31-32)

Contents

Foreword

Liberation Theology proclaims liberty to the exploited masses of Latin America. Its spirit is gradually spreading across the Western world, and creating intense discussion along with Vatican concern.

But until the first decisive act of this Theology is to "liberate" itself from exploitation by Marxism, its message will be hollow and its words will lack all power to attain the announced goal of lifting the poor and oppressed into some control of their own destiny.

This was the message of Pope John Paul II to his Liberationists at Puebla, Mexico, in January, 1979. The Pope said, in effect, you cannot free others until you first shake off your own self-imposed shackles of an alien ideology! And when you do, you will see that genuine liberation springs only from the Truth of God!

That is also the theme of this book.

Only a theology which is itself radically liberated by the Word of God is radical enough to "proclaim liberty throughout all the land unto all the inhabitants thereof" (Lev. 25:10)!

There has long been such a radical theology, and in practice it has wrested liberty from the hands of tyrants to endow the Western world with democracy and unparalleled progress. It is a practical theology drawn simply and wholly from the inspired Word of God.

This is the Word which can and will, duly preached, infuse liberating power into socio-political injustice and economic exploitation in Latin America and elsewhere. This is why its proclamation is strictly restrained in Communist totalitarian states and controlled by tyrannies of the right.

History is woven with the warp of time and woof of words. The critical choice facing mankind is a choice between following the words of Marxist or other ideology or obedience to the Word of God.

This book is aimed at clarifying that choice.

Introduction

Liberation Theology is the latest of a series of labels applied to what is essentially the same entity. It has been called Political Theology, and Theology of Revolution, and Revolutionary Theology en route to acquiring the Liberation label most commonly used in Latin (that is Central and South) America. As Political Theology its most prominent advocates are the Catholic Johannes Metz and Protestant Jürgen Moltmann in Germany; as Revolutionary Theology its best known representative is Richard Shaull in the USA; and as Liberation Theology it is urged upon the world by Catholic priests, with some Protestant collaboration, largely in Latin America.

These are the main streams of what Liberationists like to call "theological reflection." There are innumerable tributaries and countless bits of flotsam and jetsam joining the LT stream (we will often use LT for Liberation Theology for convenience)—and lots of eddies in the swirling current itself. Because this is so, some Liberationists try to blunt criticism by stressing their differences. But we observe that Liberation Theologians are given to talking of themselves as "we," and "us," and "our," and rarely explicitly reject each other's "reflections," implying enough concensus to legitimize treating Liberation Theology as an entity. The differences granted, there remains a central core which is our subject here.

Liberation Theology takes its structure from Marxism. It does so by rejecting the authority of the Bible and at the cost of ten basic Christian doctrines. Real hope for justice resides only in total commitment to the Word of God. To develop these theses we proceed as follows:

1) A brief outline of Marxism, and its functioning as an ideology.

2) An examination of Liberation Theology to show that it chooses to be defined by Marxism and quite willingly exchanges both the Bible and ten basic Christian doctrines for Marxist collaboration.

3) Finally, by contrast, a brief account of the constructive historical consequences derived by the West from the Word of God courageously

preached—to show that in the Truth, as John Paul said, throbs the power for genuine socio-political liberation.

We have chosen to illustrate what we say of LT through copious quotations from writers who identify themselves as Liberationists. They are listed alphabetically in the bibliography. Each book has its own identifying number, and reference to it in our text is made by that number plus the number of the page being quoted.

We conclude with a study guide composed of a summary and questions designed to promote insight into the subject and to open horizons for discussion and individual judgment.

PART I

What Is Marxism?

These two great discoveries, the materialistic conception of history and the revelation of the secret of capitalist production through surplus value, we owe to Marx. With these discoveries socialism became a science.

Frederich Engels

The great scientific service rendered by Marx is this, that he regarded man's nature itself as the eternally changing result of historical progress, the cause of which lies outside man. . . . while man, to maintain his existence, acts on the external world, he changes his own nature.

Georgi Plekhanov

What I did that was new was to prove: (1) that the existence of classes is only bound up with particular historical phases in the development of production, (2) that the class struggle necessarily leads to the dictatorship of the proletariat, and (3) that this dictatorship itself only constitutes the transition to the abolition of all classes and to a classless society.

Karl Marx

1

The Goal of Marxism

The goal of Marxism is the creation of a "new" man in a classless society.

The simplest key to Marxism is *The Communist Manifesto* (bibl. item 56—hereafter simply item number and where applicable page number), written jointly by Marx and Engels in 1847 and published by the Communist League of London in February, 1848. Written in a heady, inflammatory style, the *Manifesto* has illumined countless barricades with the lurid flames of rebellion.

With the *Manifesto* as our guide, and the first volume of Marx's *Capital* (54) as our basic resource, we can profile the essence of Marxism in a series of four statements which we will call "pillars." Having examined these, we will show how Liberation Theology chooses to structure itself upon these same Marxist pillars.

Marx had no intention of doing, or founding, theology. He was stubbornly atheistic, and had a distinct distaste for religion.

In rejecting Christianity and the God of his own Hebrew ancestry, Karl Marx knew precisely what he was doing. He was, he thought, liberating man from a baneful illusion which man had foisted upon himself. But this surely means that to be authentic any effort to fuse Marxism and Christianity must first of all dispose of . . . Marx! To make Marx a "convert," even a half-convert, you must first take him for a fool. Not much of a recommendation, neither of Marxism nor of whatever amalgam is attempted!

Marx was ethnically Jewish. He knew it, and occasionally took note of anti-Semitism.

Karl's lineage, on the side of both his parents, can be traced back through an ancestry of Jewish rabbis. The Old Testament dwelt in the Marxs' genes. Though Karl's father Heinrich was a lawyer, and even "went over" to Lutheranism when Karl was seven, the spirituality of the rabbinate flowed in Karl's blood. Every now and then the passion of the Hebrew prophets blazes out of Marx's often turgid style in blistering denunciation of human injustice. But Marx never mounts his prophetic indignation in the name of God.

The distinguished Anglo-Catholic historian, Christopher Dawson, somewhere calls Marx "the last of the Hebrew prophets." A characterization true enough to Marx's burning hunger for righteousness, but he was a prophet, then, in the name of humanity rather than in the name of God. And, unlike God, humanity has played Marx false.

There are those who are fond of constructing a doctrinal parallel to Christianity out of Marxism: 1) paradise is, in Marx, the original primitive, undifferentiated society; 2) man's Fall, in Marx, came (as Engels himself put it) when the first man claimed a piece of productive property (perhaps an oak tree, or bow and arrow) as exclusively "mine!"; 3) the sad history of depravity resulting from the Fall takes the form of exploitation and all the evils arising out of class struggle; 4) the proletariat emerges as the "suffering savior" of mankind; 5) the last judgment will come when the worldwide proletariat brings down capitalist civilization through violent revolution; 6) heaven follows in the form of the classless society. It's probably a fancy which Marx might have found amusing—but suggests that Marx did project a secular soteriology (doctrine of salvation).

Let's just remember that Marx very consciously opted for atheism, and did so to found man's hopes for the future on an innate and independent capacity for self-redemption. Marx consciously stressed an intrinsic incompatibility between his atheistic secularism and the "infantilism" of religion, holding that the dawn of his own "scientific" approach sheds a light of certainty which faith only gropes for, making faith for modern man a childishly outmoded fantasy.

It is a form of intellectual chic nowadays to seek common ground between Christianity and Marxism. Marxists seem pleased to accept Christian cooperation in their own schemes for social redemption, while some Christians seem to think it an ecumenical achievement to make pilgrimages to the Soviet Union correlative to fitting the Bible with Marxist blinders. But for the "prophet" himself a hybrid "Christian" Marxism or "Marxist" Christianity would have been a mongrel devoid of social potency.

For the powerful genius of Karl Marx the only amalgam possible between Christianity and his dialectical materialism would be one in which the material throttled the spiritual. So it does, as we shall see, in Liberation Theology.

Authentic Marxism is atheistic, on purpose. Authentic Christianity is theistic, on purpose! Between these twain heaven and hell find their stations, and no dialogical dexterity will make them one!

Marxism comes to the world, not as a religion, but specifically as a "scientific" substitute for religion, offering its own analysis of human evil and its own route to the "new man," perfecting himself in a new society.

Obstacles to Progress

Marx held that two burdens must be removed from humanity's bended back before the route to a "new" humanity could be opened. These burdens removed, mankind could enter upon an era of boundless progress and development.

The first burden to be sloughed off was the illusion of God; the second, the "legal fiction" of private property.

Note well the contrast between the twin burdens which Marx wanted to lift from mankind's shoulders and that burden which weighted down "Christian" in Bunyan's classic *Pilgrim's Progress.* Bunyan's "Christian," the reader may recall, staggered under the burden of his sins until his pack tumbled into the empty tomb vacated by the Pilgrim's risen Lord (14:44)!

One does well to bear this absolute antithesis between Marxism and Christianity in mind, we repeat (one which Marx himself—who read Bunyan—would have emphasized), if he is tempted to join in the varieties of Christian-Marxist "dialogue" which seek to "heal the wound of my people lightly, saying 'Peace, peace,' when there is no peace" (Jer. 6:14; 8:11)!

Jesus, the Hebrew, and Marx, the Hebrew, had this one thing in common: neither promised peace upon the earth (Matt. 10:34). Those who would heal wounds lightly in their names do justice to neither!

Happily, however, as Marx read him, the German Lutheran theologian Ludwig Feuerbach had made recourse to the empty tomb unnecessary, had indeed re-read the Bible to refashion Christianity itself into a form of atheism.

In a word, Feuerbach had, in Marx's judgment, conclusively rid man of the burden of God in his book titled (oddly enough) *Essence of Christianity* (32). Here Feuerbach demonstrates, Marx believes, that over the ages man himself created the idea of God, where in fact no God ever was. Still worse, under the mischievous manipulation of priesthoods, man "alienated" to this illusory construction the very best of his own talents.

God became a vampire, sucking from the human race the faith in its own capacities requisite to true progress. Religion thus cripples mankind into an abject servitude.

Man had indolently alienated the best of his power, of his intelligence, of his hopes and of his virtues to a myth, a *persona*, really of his own imaginary creation. God had not made man; man had made 'God.' Religious man has groveled before a fiction. Who could redeem man from this illusion, and thus liberate man for the full development of his own talents?

Who saves man? Feuerbach asks. Of course, Jesus Christ does that, properly understood, Feuerbach answers, quoting widely from the New Testament in an exegesis all his own. Feuerbach's Christ comes to redeem man from the incubus of illusion by showing that all of us are—if only we "believe"—"sons" of God just as Jesus was a Son of God. Jesus teaches those who truly understand Him that God's "attributes" are in fact but human attributes, too long alienated to a fiction. Christ reveals man to himself.

That is the secret, Feuerbach holds, of what the Church calls "redemption in Christ!" Man can be god to his own future, once he perceives that the "God" he has mistakenly created in the skies dwells within.

The "Christian" message for modern man, then, is this: undo the "alienation" of our own potential to the emptiness of the blue, get religion and the religious off our backs, and make of history a temple to the glory of mankind!

Religion joins the fossils in museums once called churches—a transition later physically accomplished in the Soviet Union.

With this invigorating philosophy, Feuerbach, Marx concludes, shatters the first of the two illusive barricades to endless progress.

Marx intends to shatter the other!

If Feuerbach dissolves the alienation implicit in religion, there remains man's alienation from himself and his own kind. Even men destined to make themselves as gods are not yet free.

How is mankind divided against itself?

This is the question Marx set himself to answer, and a division Marx set himself to resolve.

Mankind is alienated from itself, Marx believed, by all the evils men do to each other. And while Christianity attributes evil-doing to its source in man's inherited disposition to sin, Marx comes to attribute all personal and social evil to the class struggle foisted upon history through the private ownership of the means of production. In short, the source of human alienation in all its aspects is not innate; it is a system of economic relations which could be changed!

Destroy the right to private ownership of the means of production, Marx discovers, and with it will disappear all the evils men do to one another!

Marxism emerges as a form of human self-redemption!

The way to liberating humanity from the second barrier to progress will not be as easy as just reading Feuerbach. History itself must be changed! In his famous eleventh thesis on Feuerbach, Marx sets the program: "The philosophers have only interpreted the world; the point is to *change* it" (58,II:403).

Ah, but that is the tantalizing challenge every social activist faces: CHANGE! How? By what force? Make men "new"—but by what alchemy?

It is the genius of Marx to have found a way to tap immense social energies focused by shrewd manipulators upon "changing" the course of history. It is here that Marxism most acutely confronts Christianity—which is also interested in changing man and his behavior. And, as we shall see, it is in pursuit of the power to change the human being that Marxism and Christianity most profoundly clash.

Marx is quoted in the minutes of the London Central Committee of the Communist League: "We say to the workers, 'You have got to go through fifteen, twenty, fifty years of civil wars and national wars not merely in order to change your conditions but in order to change yourselves and become qualified for political power' " (57:92).

This is the *messianic* message of Marxism: freed of the illusion of God, men can align themselves with the forces of history to renovate the human race. To illumine the pilgrimage of mankind with this option is Marx's understanding of his role in history. "Change yourselves!" You can become *new* men through rebellion and the classless society! It is a theme which echoes in the official Programs of the Communist Party of the Soviet Union (CPSU) to our own times.

But messianism is exclusive. There is no room for two "messiahs" in the temple of history.

If Marxism is deliberately messianic—and it is, having as its goal the making man "new"—and if Christianity is deliberately Messianic—and it is, having as its goal the making man "new"—then the Lord's stern words apply: "He who does not take his cross and follow me is not worthy of me" (Matt. 10:38).

Follow Him! Or, follow Marx! The road divides where both the Christ and Marx himself set up markers pointing in exactly opposite directions!

Marx knows, of course, that creation of the "new" depends upon recognition of what ails the "old" man. What Marx does not acknowledge is that the "old" man, fallen from the beginning in the first man, can no longer discern on his own what ails himself and mankind. Only divine revelation—which Marx knows well enough, but rejects—can do that.

Note well what is at issue: can man diagnose his own spiritual maladies, and then prescribe his own cure? Or is the inherited taint, as Christianity teaches, so pervasive that man is blinded from the start to the cause of his alienation from both God and his fellows?

Marx's position, and that of many world religions and of Western humanism is that man *can* diagnose the cause of personal and social evil, and having done so, *can* both propose and effect the necessary cure.

The position of Christianity is that only divine revelation can shed true light into the labyrinth of the soul to illumine the root of sin and evil; and that faith in the redemptive mission of Jesus Christ, as revealed in the Scriptures, can inaugurate a lifelong process of spiritual and social renovation. Christianity embraces person, society and world!

The choice forced upon the world by Marxism is between the words of Marx and the Word of God.

That choice is at issue also as between Liberation Theology and Christian orthodoxy—and it is what this book is all about.

To move along, we can, for purposes of clarity, outline the essence of Marx's system in a series of four propositions, which we will call the "pillars" of Marxism. We will then show that these same four pillars have been lifted from Marx to structure Liberation Theology.

2

The Four Pillars of Marxism

1. Class Struggle

Marx denies that evil is natural to mankind. We are not born bad, nor with a proclivity to evil. Human evil is an imposition upon human society by the savagery of social relations molded by class struggle.

This must be clearly understood. Man is not, Marx holds, as traditional Christianity teaches, born "depraved" by heritage from his fallen first parents, Adam and Eve. This "slander" on the human race was dismissed to what Leon Trotsky was fond of calling "the dustbin of history" by the researches of Feuerbach.

But if, in fact, everyone agrees that man is not quite what he ought to be, from whence the faults that make him so—if the Fall and inherited depravity be denied?

Marx discerns the origin of evil in class struggle. What ails human nature is imposed upon us from the outside: the all-encompassing class struggle.

Most of us, it is true, are unaware of involvement in any class struggle. Struggle? With whom? And how?

That is what Marx was born to teach us!

For it is just this struggle, Marx holds, which is the source of all the murder, malice, hatred and every other crime that human beings inflict upon each other and upon themselves. His own "scientific" analysis of human history demonstrates to Marx's satisfaction that at the root of man's alienation from man is not depravity but class struggle.

Note well that Marx shrewdly emphasizes *class* struggle.

And what defines the classes engaged in this internecine warfare?

According to Marx, class struggle is waged across the centuries between society's "haves" and "have-nots," who are divided by what Marx calls "relations of production." And the "relations of production" revolve around one absolute distinction: the distinction between those (few) who *own* the means of production and those (many) who must *sell* (or give under the duress of slavery) their labor-power (that is, themselves!) to survive.

Here, Marx thinks, a "scientific" analysis of social structures lays its finger upon what Christianity mistakenly thinks of as inherited human depravity. The source of all evil, personal and social, is quite simply class struggle. This, Marx says, was common knowledge by his own time:

"No credit is due me for discovering the existence of classes in modern society or the struggle between them. Long before me bourgeois historians had described the historical development of this class struggle and bourgeois economists the economic anatomy of the classes" (57:57).

What, however, bourgeois political economy did not do was to substitute class struggle for the Fall of man as source of human evil.

Class lines are not always writ plain across the brow of history, Marx and Engels say in the *Manifesto,* but in this age of capitalism they are unmistakable: it is the capitalist-owners, or *bourgeoisie,* and the workers, or *proletariat,* who are locked in the struggle which fuels all evil and defines all social relations.

Every institution, Marx holds, reflects the power of the bourgeoisie and the impotence of the exploited proletariat. For example, what is "law," asks Marx the lawyer, but the defense of the bourgeois right to private property? And what is the role of the courts except to enforce that right? Why schools except to put trained youth on the market for the bourgeoisie to buy? Why the church but to teach that wealth is proof of divine blessing, and that the poor are to accept their lot as divinely ordained? The police, reinforced when necessary by the militia, protect the exploitative system; and the military keep out foreign intervention. The arts extol the winners, and recreation is only for those able to afford it—the bourgeoisie. All society reeks, Marx thinks, with the blood, sweat and toil—and the tinsel, extravagance and greed—of class struggle.

But, in fact, class struggle leaves neither class uncorrupted. Blinded by their gross materialism, the bourgeoisie grow hard and indifferent to human suffering; consumed by pain and envy, the proletariat become ever more bitter at their plight. Man's very humanity is the victim of economic relations which inevitably set a minority class over a majority class—with no resolution in sight unless the root of the struggle be traced, isolated and done away. Meanwhile, all the evils society suffers, Marx insists, draw their nourishment from the struggle between these classes, the struggle which defines, as it underlies, the social structure.

First pillar of Marxism, then: all society is warped by class struggle, the true source of human evil.

2. Private Property

But why a class struggle? Why any struggle at all?

What, really, has private property to do with it?

By private property Marx does not mean the personal ownership of toothbrushes, wearing apparel, or, even if there were enough of them, motor cars. These may spell comfort, and excite envy, but are not the root of class struggle.

The private ownership Marx has in view is that of the *means of production*—the factories, the mines, utilities, communications, finance, the heart of what is called capitalism.

Why is such ownership, then, productive of class struggle?

Because control of these empower the bourgeoisie to exploit the proletariat. Without any resources save their labor power, the "proles" must appear on the market as commodities for sale at market price, that is at the going wage. This is the terrible, life and death power that private ownership confers upon a small class of often ruthless entrepeneurs. And it is to ensure such bourgeois dominance that the whole institutional superstructure of society—as we have already seen—is organized.

For Marx, the very term "proletariat" denotes those who must sell their labor power, which is themselves, in order to survive. Indeed, the moral fervor which betimes flashes out of Marx's *Capital* rises from a blazing indictment of a system which Marx views as making the worker just another commodity, born and raised and trained to be bought at the going wage.

It is himself, in the form of labor power, that the worker sells lest he and his family die. It is himself, in the form of work accomplished and products produced, that the worker is stripped of in exchange for a pay check, which Marx calls "the cash nexus"—a check which always rewards him for less than he produces so that the capitalist can realize a profit.

Marxism becomes clearer when we realize that central to it are two theories, the first of which Marx freely admits deriving from others:

a) *The labor theory of value,* namely that all the value to be found in any product inheres in the labor invested in its making (or in the making of the machines that produce it); English economists had long taught this. A crucial correlative upon which Marx insists is that all labor, be it of head or hand, is of equal worth.

b) Marx's own contribution, *the theory of surplus value,* is his contention that the only way in which the capitalist can realize a profit on his investment is by paying labor for less than labor produces. This is the crux of Marxism. Capitalism means the investment of money for the realization of profit in money. But Aristotle had long ago pointed out, Marx notes, that "money is sterile and produces no offspring." This means that capital by itself turns no profit. Mere money could lie dormant for centuries—and not increase itself by one cent! How, then, can the capitalist realize a profit on his investment *except* labor, which alone creates value, be paid for less than the market worth of what it produces?

But payment for less than one takes is, in a word, *theft.* However "legal" such thievery may be made by legislatures, and enforced by courts, both corrupted in favor of the bourgeoisie, in fact it is this universal iniquity which fuses class struggle. The proletariat are forever pursuing "justice," the bourgeoisie are forever keeping their "wage slaves" in place.

From these twin theses, then, of *labor theory of value* and *theory of surplus value,* Marx erects his indictment of capitalism as source of class struggle, root of man's exploitation of man, and hence source of all evil both social and personal.

Second pillar of Marxism, then: class struggle occasioned by the legal right (which Marx thinks a legal fiction) to private ownership of the means of production.

3. The Cure: Violent Rebellion

Having diagnosed the cause of human depravity, Marx moves on to the cure—his cure. Just as Feuerbach has relieved mankind of the burden of God, so Marx proposes to relieve mankind of the burden of evil. How?

By cutting the root of class struggle and its resulting inhumanities, that root being the private ownership of productive means. This burden to be lifted via a rebellion aimed to destroy the social institutions which protect capitalism.

Because, as we have seen, the right to private property is so profoundly entrenched in the socio-political system erected to protect it, Marx is persuaded that the only way to break its sinister influence is to bring down the whole capitalist system, top to bottom—state, industry, business, church, school, legal system, bourgeois morality and art . . . everything!

This calls for rebellion!

While some Marxists (like Eduard Bernstein and the later Karl Kautsky, scorned by the purists as "revisionists" or "reformists") held that Marxism could enter history (as Communism) by way of parliamentary election, mainline Marxism anticipates only violent rebellion as the gateway to tomorrow. The class struggle is too bitter, the gulf between bourgeoisie and proletariat too fundamental, for bridging in any peaceful way. The capitalist system must be smashed! Not only must rebellion be mounted, but after its initial success there must be an interim—the "dictatorship of the proletariat"—when the rebel vanguard will dismantle, piece by piece, the last remnants of the bourgeois world.

Eventually, Marx held, and Lenin theorized in his *State And Revolution* (50), the state will "wither away," and all political and economic decisions will be made by committees of the proletariat. Gradually society will become struggle free, and true communism will appear: from each according to his ability, and to each according to his need.

Evil joins the dinosaurs and the churches as outmoded by history—a transition the Soviet Union has by no means achieved!

Third pillar of Marxism, then: overthrow of the capitalist system through violent proletarian rebellion.

4. The New Man

Having diagnosed the malady of the "old" man, Marx can prescribe the process for making man himself "new."

In fact, the prescription has in fact been made: through the revolution, and under the interim dictatorship of the proletariat, a new kind of man must emerge! So Marxism holds. He is the kind of man who is liberating himself by taking his destiny into his own hands.

Leon Trotsky, who with Lenin brought off the Russian Revolution of 1917 and saw it to permanence, muses in his *Literature And Revolution* what that Marxist "new man" will be like:

"Through the machine, man in socialist society will command nature in its entirety," Trotsky writes, "with its grouse and its sturgeons. He will point out places for mountains and for passes. He will change the course of the rivers, and he will lay down rules for oceans. . . . Man will become immeasurably stronger, wiser and subtler; his body will become more harmonized, his movements more rhythmic, his voice more musical. The forms of life will become dynamically dramatic. The average human type will rise to the heights of an Aristotle, a Goethe, or a Marx. And above this ridge new peaks will rise" (86:252, 256).

And in his "last will and testament," written but a few months before Stalin's agent tricked his way into Trotsky's confidence and brutally murdered him, Trotsky writes: "Life is beautiful. Let the future generations cleanse it of all evil, oppression, and violence, and enjoy it to the full" (22:479).

Fourth pillar of Marxism, then: man makes himself "new" through revolution and its consequent classless society.

5. Summary

In a famous letter to German socialist Georg Wedemeyer, written 5 March, 1852, Marx summarizes his work to that time: "No credit is due me for discovering the existence of classes in modern society or the struggle between them . . . What I did that was new was to prove: (1) that the existence of classes is only bound up with particular historical phases in the development of production, (2) that the class struggle necessarily leads to the dictatorship of the proletariat, and (3) that this dictatorship itself only constitutes the transition to the abolition of all classes and to a classless society" (57:57).

Whether or not Marxism be called a secular gospel, Marx certainly intended to proclaim an analysis of, and cure for, human evil, and to single out the energy and the process man needs to make himself new.

Marx intends, quite consciously, to make Christianity superfluous.

The Church has, he thinks, failed over eighteen centuries to re-*new* mankind. Feuerbach has shown why; Marx will show how the job can be done.

But can authentic Marxism, then, be united with Christianity? Liberationists of various hues think so, as do some theologians. Marxism affords, they think, the working tool to achieve ends they themselves seek in the name of the Gospel. But the rental of that tool comes high! It will, as we shall see, cost the essence of Christianity.

PART II

Why *Not* Marxism?

In accepting its aims, we accepted what was the height of egoism, inhumanity, economic nonsense, insult to human nature, and destruction of human liberty—but none of this bothered us a bit.

Fyodor Dostoevsky

Tyranny is a habit; once rooted, it grows like a disease. I am firmly of the opinion that the best man in the world can grow coarse and insensitive from habit to a point where he becomes indistinguishable from a wild beast. Blood and power intoxicate: they lead to callousness and depravity; the most abnormal phenomena become accessible and, finally, enjoyable mentally and emotionally.

Fyodor Dostoevsky

How would you have dared tell anybody that the idea of the (economic) basis and the (social) superstructure was an absurd piece of dogmatism?

Nahdezhda Mandelstam

3

Where Can You Ask That Question?

Why *not* Marxism?

Well, in a word, because wherever Marxism prevails you cannot ask that question!

Maybe you should read that twice, to let its implication soak in!

That's more than ground enough for anyone who wants freedom, not only for himself but for others, to reject Marxism out of hand.

There are those, of course, (and they are many!) who say that Marxism does not *necessarily* mean the totalitarian state. But were they correct, then Marx misled himself, for it is he (as we have already heard) who claims *proving* that "the class struggle necessarily leads to the dictatorship of the proletariat" (57:57)! Take note, Marx is not saying "may," or "could," or "might" but "*necessarily* leads . . . !"

Marxism divorced from dictatorship is not Marxism! The dialectical materialism which Marx developed leads inevitably to dictatorship! Marx himself formulated the system that way!

And because Marx did indeed open the door of history to some of the most thorough, and brutal, forms of dictatorship mankind has yet endured, that telltale question, "Why a 'No' to Marxism?" can only be asked where Marxism is *not* already in political power! Even such visitors to the Soviet Union as those who come back praising what they have seen, never heard a Russian ask: "Why . . . ?" And probably never asked it themselves.

And so the question answers itself! "Why Not Marxism?"—just because under Marxism that question cannot be raised. You don't ask, unless hankering after an interview with the security police, "Why . . . anything?" in Marxist societies.

Whoever needs more persuasive reason for rejecting Marxism does not understand, or does not fully appreciate, the meaning of freedom.

For all but the most myopic of citizens, the fact that you *can* ask, any time and anywhere, "Why democracy?" under the very protection of democracy ought to clinch the answer to: Why Democracy Instead of Marxism?

Democracy is far from perfect, but the key to progressive change is in freedom for self-criticism, a freedom which democracy protects and Communism prohibits. Try a little reading in the accounts written by victims of Marxist "justice" (see our bibliography, items 24, 25, 49, 52, 53, 79, for example) if you want to breathe the air of freedom with greater exhilaration.

Bear in mind, as we now take a look at Marxism in greater detail, that a society which forbids asking, "Why . . ?" is one which undermines every human relationship by calling every association and every value "political"—and tyrannizing over them all!

We say "NO" to Marxism because it entails, quite consciously and deliberately, a dictatorial state in which the merest hint of deviation, the "suspicion of being suspect" is enough to commit you to prison, to exile or to death!

4

What About the Four Pillars?

But what might be said about the four pillars of Marxism? Whatever they lead to, are they in themselves sound socio-economics?

A glance at a library card catalog will show that each of the four pillars has long since Marx been bathed in torrents of critical printer's ink. Library shelves overflow with books which either promote or demote the four pillars. This much may be said here to suggest a perspective:

1. Class Struggle a Slogan

We will show in the following chapter that class struggle is a propaganda slogan, not a "scientific" description of social relations now or ever before.

The source of the evils which plague mankind is within the human soul. The struggles which occur among peoples and between nations are symptoms of innate depravity. The very use of slogans like "class struggle" to mislead by masquerading as truth is also a symptom of human perversity.

2. Private Property Biblical

The right to private property is biblical ("You shall not steal!") and has been proclaimed by the Church across the ages. That this right, like all rights, is widely abused, points to innate depravity, not to rebellion.

And Marxism has shown the world that when rebellion does displace the current owners of productive property it simply replaces them with commissars usually more ruthless, and often far less competent, than the private owners were. Moreover experience has indubitably demonstrated that production under private ownership capitalism far exceeds that under Communism in quantity and far excels it in quality.

The chains of exploitation which Marx so vividly portrays and denounces in *Capital* (54) are most efficiently forged in the so-called "Peoples' " Republics created by Marxism. Indeed, many a prominent member of some Chamber of Commerce in the West no doubt secretly envies the absence of "labor troubles" so effectively provided by the secret police in the East.

The fact that Marx and Engels, and a whole host of others, could so freely expose economic evils in the Western world led to massive efforts at reform, including the growth of the free labor movement. But for a Marx or Engels or anyone else to criticize from within the Communist state monopolies today would mean the Gulag or death.

Economics is the science of building a bridge between world resources and human needs. As Michael Novak persuasively argues in his *The Spirit of Democratic Capitalism* (77), that bridge is built most efficiently and carries the largest cargo of goods under precisely the capitalistic structure which Marx attacked—even when its most vocal Marxist critics leave off enjoying its fruits long enough to denounce it.

In brief, private ownership of productive means does not produce "class struggle," and is not the root of personal or social evil. And whatever private ownership's many abuses, the Marxist alternative only multiplies them.

3. Revolution Not Rebellion

We will distinguish rebellion from revolution in the following chapter, and show why Marxist rebellion leads inevitably to dictatorship, as indeed Marx said it would.

4. Man Cannot Produce the "New" Man

No one seems satisfied with man as he is.

Schemes for re-doing the human race divide along one chasm: is human imperfection due to social structures, which man could change to achieve his own renovation? Or are imperfect social structures but the reflection of imperfect human beings, who themselves must be changed?

That comparison between man made "new" through a rebellion which brutally transforms social relationships, and man made "new" in Christ as the source of progressive social evolution is implicit throughout this study. We will draw out the contrast as we proceed.

In brief, can we redeem ourselves by overthrowing exploitative relations of production? Was Marx, standing on the shoulders of Feuerbach, a far-seeing prophet?

Or does the world's experience, since 1917, of Communist states, where Marxism has taken historical configuration, suggest that when unredeemed men take dictatorial power to make other men "new," the result is not the end of struggle but rather the onset of endless tragedy?

Whatever the "class struggle" tensions in Russia, Cuba, China and other Communist states were before Marxism came, they have been violently multiplied by the application of Marx's "cure." Whatever the pre-revolutionary oppression of the many by the few in these countries, exploitation is now absolute! Whatever the fear, the insecurity, the restriction of personal freedom before Communism, all are now intensified! However large the number of those tortured and executed before the revolution, that sinister figure has been grotesquely multiplied. More there may be of physical amenities, of strictly indoctrinating schooling, of access to health care—among those who escape the purges—in some Communist states, yes; but only to accent the lesson among the victims of the tyranny that "man does not live by bread alone" (Luke 4:4; quoting Deut. 8:3).

For all his genius, Marx was mistaken!

Man does not recover the "life" lost through sin in the Garden of Eden by way of further rebellion! Animal comforts, even if multiplied, only counterfeit genuine liberation. No proletariat has ever emerged from the violence of rebellion as new creatures vying for sainthood—how vividly the the daily news testifies to that!

Yet the "conversion" of countless millions to Marxist ideology, and their subsequent subjugation by Communist tyranny now fuel the sharpest and most dangerous international tensions in today's world.

These tensions are exacerbated in Latin America by the strident voices of the Liberation Theologians.

5. Summary

Marxism in practice, whatever the utopian dreams of Marx and Engels, functions, despite its pretensions to "science," as just one more scheme for bringing the unscrupulous to political power—-tyrants who, once enthroned in the seat of the mighty, *never* submit their rule to popular referendum. Can you think of one Communist country where it has been otherwise?

Marx was fond of saying that "praxis," that is results, was the final test of the truth of any theory. By that test, the four pillars of Marxism fall far short of the truth about man, his past and his future.

But Marxism seduces, in fact, not because it is science but because it is an ideology. Liberation Theology follows the same route.

Let us trace how that goes.

5

Marxism Is an Ideology

Marxism is an ideology.

Once grasped, this fact provides some explanation for the baleful impact which Marxism, taking political form as Communism, has upon history.

Liberation Theology is an ideology too.

So let us ask:

1. What Is Ideology?

An *ideology* has something to do, obviously, with an idea.

An *ideologue* is one who develops and exploits an ideology.

An ideology begins as someone's idea. Marxism, of course, begins with the ideas of Karl Marx—and Frederich Engels.

To become an ideology, the idea must be expanded into a system. But not just any system. An ideology is designed to stimulate action. Successful ideologies push history around, unsheath swords. Powerful ideologies, like Marxism and Fascism, set lips to shouting, turn crowds into mobs and sometimes bathe streets in blood. This is what ideologies are for. They seem to drive history close to the golden sun—and fall scorched into disaster.

Marxism is an ideology; so is Fascism. LT obviously aspires to be another, developed along Marxist lines. There are lots of lesser ideologies, pushing and shoving people around at all social levels. You will see them at work in business, politics, church and school—ideas become weapons to coerce others.

Just how do ideologies generate action?

They begin by dreaming aloud of goals beyond the horizon—the classless society, the thousand year Reich, a perfect educational system, the pure church. . . . Always irresistible to those not solidly rooted in convictions of their own. Always irresistible, too, to those who want to believe that they cannot be responsible for their own frustrations. In a word, ideology always masquerades as "liberating!"

Marx and Engels had views on ideology, though they never thought of themselves, or of their system, as ideological.

Said Engels, "To construct conclusions in one's head, take them as a basis from which to start, and then reconstruct the world from them in one's head is *ideology*" (31:464).

Said Marx, "Ideology is a process accomplished by a so-called thinker, consciously indeed, but with a false consciousness. The real motives impelling him remain unknown to him, otherwise it would not be an ideological process at all . . . [he] never passes outside the sphere of thought" (57:511-12).

Both agree that an ideology is a function of an idea. And both agree in Marx's judgment that an ideology functions to obscure the ideologue's real motives, it may be not only from others but also from himself. Marx, for example, thought that bourgeois ideology clothes the economic roots of social relations in the misleading garb of abstract notions, like democracy, liberty, justice, equality, etc. Counting their work as "scientific," rather than ideological, Marx and Engels thought to brush ideology aside. Theirs is, none-the-less, the dominant ideology of our era.

2. Ideology Stifles Conscience

All ideologies share a common factor, and perform a common service, one which ideologues never mention: *ideology stifles conscience!*

Ideology has no more important historical impact!

Neither Engels nor Marx seems to notice how neatly ideology conspires to silence the voice of God in history: the human conscience!

Consider: Stalin murders millions of Russian peasants. His Marxist ideology blesses the bloodbath as essential to integrating agriculture into a stable Soviet economy! Conscience, be gone! Again, Lenin forges political agreements, both internal and external, which he never intends to keep. The lie becomes, and has remained, an instrument of Soviet policy. Conscience, be gone!

Every ideology creates its own (im)morality, and justifies it against every twinge of conscience: all yields to the whim of the idea!

Murder? Does conscience witness, "Thou shalt not kill?" Ideology exonerates killing as essential to the realization of *the* Idea!

War? Ideology blesses as "peace" by other means.

Betrayal? Rids the cause of a traitor to *the* Idea!

Falsehood? Sets the enemy of *the* Idea off on a misleading scent.

Deception? Theft? Promises made to be broken? Not so much approved as mandated by *the* Idea!

Morality, then? Measured, not by conscience or law, but exclusively by what promotes *the* Idea—always as decided by the ruling ideologue.

No mendacity, trickery, betrayal or outrage has in practice ever exhausted the capacity of ideology to justify and bless.

Ideology inscribes its visions on the sky and upon the heart, and drowns the voice of conscience in the roar of the mob.

Ideology and Christianity bestride opposite poles in world history.

Marxism *is* an ideology. So is Liberation Theology!

3. Ideology and Class Struggle

We can now perceive that "class struggle" is but a propaganda slogan forged by Marxist ideology.

"Class struggle" simply focuses the hatred of a society's discontented upon a ruling authority the ideologue wants to replace—with himself!

But what in fact is *class struggle?*

Marxism proclaims class struggle, we have noted, as descriptive of things as they are, at least in capitalist countries. Have you ever noticed that no Marxist talks about class struggle in the terrible tensions of Communist states? Having done its lethal work, the slogan is discarded!

Evil is, indeed, real enough; so real as to cost the suffering and death of God's own Son! Exploitation is an awesomely prevalent thing. And the plight of the poor in Latin America does cry to heaven for alleviation.

Our contention with Marxism and Liberation Theology is over how to confront the deplorable circumstances all acknowledge. Our response, validated by history, is proposed in the last section of this study.

No resolution of economic injustice and social imbalance begins with the imposition of the theory of class struggle upon Latin America. Because "class struggle" is only a slogan!

This is evidenced by the fact, already noted, that "class struggle" is never mentioned by Marxist/LT theorists as regards Communist states. But everything that Marx attributed to class struggle abounds in Communist societies—hatred, envy, murder, corruption, dishonesty—yet no ideologist ever adduces class struggle as the cause!

Why not?

Because for Marxism/LT "class struggle" is not descriptive; it is propaganda!

Ask yourself: is it not strange that so real, pervasive and influential a strife as Marx claims class struggle to be must be *taught* to almost all whose whole lives are supposed to be governed by it? Could you, for example, describe right now, not the pain life imposes upon you, but just how the personal and social relationships which pattern your day reflect your role in class struggle?

In truth, "class struggle" is a slogan which incites you for the first time to look upon a certain group of others (most of whom you do not even know) as your enemies! For some it becomes a convenient short-cut to blaming a whole "class" of strangers for their problems. And, if you take the bait, you will do, and approve doing, violence against others as members of a "class," which you would never do against them as individuals. The slogan has taken you in, and set a finger to the lips of conscience.

Because a "class" is very loosely defined, its elimination will be haphazard and often excessive. Even Lenin soon concluded that the Russian Revolution had far too carelessly slaughtered those whose gifts for management were indispensable to progress—and did all he could to tempt business experts back to Russia. Professor Adam Ulam, noted Sovietologist of Harvard writes in his highly instructive book *The Bolsheviks,*

"The experience of War Communism caused Lenin to make a belated discovery: the capitalist was not only a valuable specialist; he was also possessor of some magic gift that the 'heroic proletarian' completely lacked and that could not be learned by reading Marx and Engels. Lenin's praise not only of capitalism, which is normal for a Marxist, but of the *capitalist* now became so extravagant that it would sound embarrassingly excessive in the mouth of a president of an American Chamber of Commerce. 'The capitalists know how to provide goods and you don't know how,' he told the last Party Congress he attended in 1922. He bewailed the extinction of the breed in Russia. . . . Karl Marx wrote about everything else, he bewailed, but there is not a word in his writings about how 'state capitalism can coexist with communism' " (87:482-83). The slogan of "class struggle" with its correlative of "class enemy" had worked too well in 1917.

Class struggle is not a description; it is propaganda. Class struggle is a revolutionary slogan, cleverly designed to focus hatred for purposes of inciting reaction.

Injustice there is, all around the world and in our own backyards. Marxism *uses* it, almost gleefully—and so does LT!—to focus the pain of injustice upon the elimination of an "enemy class." But experience has taught the world—or ought to teach the world—that when the presumedly exploiting "class" is destroyed, a far more ruthless "class" takes its place—what Milovan Djilas, Jugoslavian Communist, calls, in his penetrating study, *The New Class* (24)!

Class struggle is a slogan which works because it is so deceptively simple; thought can stop and emotion take over with a catch phrase: we are the victims of a class which profits from our defeats! *Down with 'em!*

And it is only when the manacles of the "new class" click about our wrists that we awake to realize having been duped!

Brandishing the banner of "class struggle," ideology uses its deluded victims first as its warriors and then as its victims.

In the Marxist ideological genre, Liberation Theology strives now to "conscienticize" a suffering peasantry to view their plight as caused by a class enemy—for purposes of fomenting rebellion.

So ideology has betrayed its millions, as is plain for all to see, in Russia, in China, in Cuba, in Vietnam, Laos, Cambodia and wherever else the Marxist ideology has become an "historical force."

So it will be in Latin America if Liberation Theology has its way.

4. Hegel and Class Struggle

For those who are interested in the history of ideas (others may skip ahead to the next section), it is evident that Marx's use of the notion of "class struggle" reflects philosophical rather than historical roots.

Marx was thoroughly versed in, and profoundly influenced by, the philosophy of G.W.F. Hegel, a German born in 1770 who died in 1831.

It was his task, Marx often said, to set Hegelianism on its feet, a correction required by Hegel's believing that mind, rather than economic forces, guided history.

Pause, now, to ask yourself: why is the modern world different from, say, the Middle Ages? What makes history "go?"

Your question reaches for an understanding of the motive forces of history. Why is history . . . history? What makes for change from one epoch to the next? Or, for that matter, from one day to the next? What influences the human decisions that together move today into tomorrow?

Hegel had an answer, one that has influenced historiography ever since. It is his doctrine of the "dialectic." Marx adopted it. And because Marx believed that economic relations governed the course of history, his philosophy is called "dialectical materialism"—or, sometimes, "historical materialism." And it is the nature of the "dialectic" which in fact supports the notion of struggle which Marx converts into "class" struggle.

The term *dialectic* derives from the Greek. It means the give and take of discussion or argument. We derive the word "dialogue" from it.

While Hegel scholars are not all agreed, we may say somewhat simplistically that Hegel sees every historical period in a kind of argument, or struggle, with itself. This struggle elicits energy. History moves ahead, thus, on forces generated by struggle. These forces function, Hegel perceives, in three, that is in triadic, steps, or lurches (developed in Hegel's *Logic*).

Let us try to apply the dialectic to the present moment, to the world in which we live and to things as they are. We will first use Hegel's terminology, and then Marx's.

Hegel calls the present, the "thesis"—the world of today, your day and our day.

It happens, Hegel believes, that because every "thesis" is a living situation, history is ever restless. This is because the "thesis" always generates within itself certain forces of opposition. Call these, then, the "antithesis"—that is, the *anti*-thesis.

Why does a "thesis" inevitably generate its "antithesis"? Hegel's answer: that's the secret of history. We see *how,* if not *why* change occurs. Marx fashioned, out of Hegel, his own answer, which we will hear in a moment. For now, theses do evoke antitheses!

Pretty soon the antithesis comes to engage the thesis in a deadly struggle. Perhaps there are a series of strikes, local or national uprisings, a palace revolt, or a national rebellion. Whatever form the struggle takes, the result is: historical change! A new situation arises. Hegel calls it the "synthesis"—it contains remnants of both the thesis and the antithesis. This synthesis now becomes the new "thesis"—and history marches on.

Hegel had his own philosophical terminology for the motive force driving this triadic process: the action of the antithesis on the thesis he calls "negation." The anti-thesis brings down, or "negates," its thesis. Tomorrow emerges from today by way of destruction. (You see how this philosophy lends itself to theories of revolution, and indeed an Hegelian "Left" did grow out of Hegel's philosophy. It was balanced, however, by an Hegelian "Right," developing out of Hegel's view that the perfect state was to be found in the Prussia of his own time.)

However, in bringing down the thesis, the negation also destroys itself: the "negation of the negation."

The reader will note one very significant facet of this Hegelian dialectic: progress is motivated by destruction! It is negation, and again negation of the negation, that drives history ahead. A deadlier program than this could hardly be imagined, but it is one which Marx embraced, as does Liberation Theology: out of chaos, out of rebellion, good will somehow come! Nothing could be in sharper contrast to Christianity, where only out of the divine, out of life, can new life come!

To observe the Hegelian dialectic in practice, we will see what use Marx makes of it. And we will thus see how "class struggle" roots in philosophy rather than in observation of social reality.

The relations which determine both the character of the "thesis," and of the "antithesis," Marx held, are economic. This we have already noticed.

Marx's philosophy is therefore, as already pointed out, called "dialectical materialism."

The "thesis" is, for Marx, the Western world, whose economic foundation is capitalism. And, as we know, Marx holds that all of the political and social institutions characteristic of capitalism are determined by the basic relation of production—capital owns and labor works. This is the "thesis."

Now observe how, for Marx, the "thesis" inevitably generates its own anti-thesis.

In order to make a profit, you remember, capital must find workers who will accept (or starve) being paid for less than they produce—Marx's theory of surplus value (elaborated in documents which Karl Kautsky collected after Marx's death, and now published as Vol. IV of *Capital*).

Viewed as a "class," the proletariat is the creation of capital. It is, in short, the anti-thesis which moves history along through "class struggle."

The proletariat becomes for Marx the vehicle of negation, the antithesis which will in the long run bring down the thesis.

Here, then, are the ingredients which Marx views through Hegelian lenses as constituting the elements of "class struggle"—the bourgeoisie, whose world constitutes the thesis of our times; the proletariat, "the gravediggers of the bourgeoisie," whom Marx intends to unify as the anti-thesis of our times.

Marx consciously sacrifices all his brilliant prospects for financial success to educating the proletariat to their historical, antithetical role.

"Why have I never answered you," he writes on April 30, 1867, to a New York Socialist Siegfried Meyer. "Because I was perpetually hovering on the verge of the grave. Therefore I had to use *every* moment in which I was capable of work in order that I might finish the task to which I have sacrificed my health, my happiness in life and my family. I hope this explanation requires no further supplement. I laugh at the so-called 'practical' men and their wisdom. If one chose to be an ox one could of course turn one's back on the agonies of mankind and look after one's own skin. But I should have regarded myself as *unpractical* if I had pegged out without completely finishing my book, at least in the manuscript" (57: 219).

The manuscript to which Marx refers is that for the first volume of his *Capital* which apeared in 1867, the only volume to be published while Marx was alive.

Educated as to the root of its plight, imbued with hatred to steel its will to its task, the proletariat would one day, Marx believed, vindicate its own self-sacrifice by rising to "negate" the system that enslaved it. They would destroy the thesis, the system that enslaves and exploits: the negation of the negation. Out of the ashes of rebellion will inevitably come, guaranteed on Hegelian grounds really, a final synthesis, the new society, truly classless and open to boundless progress.

So Marx hoped. For that hope he recklessly expended himself and, as he says, sacrificed his devoted wife and impoverished family.

But what would he say, today, viewing the travesty which Communist totalitarianism makes of his dreams, and its "negation" of the worth of all that he surrendered his life to proclaim?

Who knows that? To justify deferment of Marx's anticipations, Communism draws on the inexhaustible bank of time: some day . . . !

Communism everywhere demonstrates that negation is not the source of genuine progress. Hegel was mistaken. But, of course, to impose this philosophical grid upon history Marx chooses to use unphilosophical language. Who would rebel for an antithesis? Or die to negate a negation? Revolutionary language must touch the heart, and so:

"Class struggle" emerges as the most successful propaganda slogan of all time—so far!

5. Ideology and Liberation

A final word on the relation of ideology to another slogan: liberation!

The bait for the ideological trap is "liberation."

Hatred focused on an "oppressor class" propels rebellion; the chimera of "liberation" lights the fuse!

"Liberation" is the gleam that illumines the swamp of agony and river of blood that ideology ushers into history.

But what does ideology mean by "liberation?"

Everyone thinks he knows, of course, until he begins trying to define precisely what it is that he wants "liberation" from, and "liberation" for. Is it freedom from all law? Imagine how lethal driving on our streets would be if there were no traffic laws! Is "liberation" from just some restraints? Then, which?

Ideology prudently leaves "liberation" vague and ill-defined, perhaps for two strategic purposes: a) no one can too precisely hold up the mirror to existing Communist societies for measuring just how much "liberation" they have (not) achieved; and, b) if well defined, then that particular concept of "liberation" might not seem quite worth the total self-sacrifice required of rebels enlisted to destroy existing order.

So, "liberation" implies something for everyone in general, but guarantees nothing for anyone in particular: the poor think they are promised abundance, the exploited taste sweet revenge; the "alienated" anticipate real acceptance, and the "isolated" are beguiled with anticipation of community—all (except the revenge) still utopian dreams which no ideology has realized and which negation (lacking all creative power) cannot, in fact, bring to birth.

All is hazy, except the immediate demand: destroy the oppressor class (and bring us to power!).

We may listen in advance to what one Liberation Theologian says about the term from which his theology takes its name:

"The notion of liberation," writes Liberation Theologian Gustavo Gutierrez, whose voice we will be hearing frequently as we go along, "emphasizes that man transforms himself by conquering his liberty throughout his existence and his history" (43:x).

Given no more content than that, "liberation" can of course be twisted to mean almost anything—or nothing!

The gullible are led to believe that liberation means quick escape from the present, even from one's self, into a "new" society, even a "new" humanity—but who spells out what such "newness" will be? You take the ideologist's word for it; and that, considering what has happened so far in countries "liberated" according to ideological formula, is far from encouraging security. Rebels are assured by the ideology of getting "control of their own destiny"—without any concrete assurance of, 1) just how that will be done, nor of, 2) what will "negate" the "dictatorship of the proletariat" over their future, or 3) what they can do with that destiny if ever it is brought under their control. The slogan is deliberately left empty of content, and thus conveniently binds the sloganeer to nothing.

"Liberation" is, like class struggle, a shibboleth, a "motivator"—designed for propaganda, not for realization.

The two slogans—class struggle and liberation—are propaganda correlatives! The useful myth of "class struggle" focuses the illusion of "liberation" upon a very definite goal: the destruction of one political system to introduce another.

Ideology, in short, is promoted by slogans, while claiming to be intensely scientific. And ideology in practice silences conscience against enormities of injustice and brutalization while boasting of liberating the oppressed and making mankind new.

There is, by contrast, a genuine *liberation,* foreshadowed by the Exodus of Israel from Egypt: it is mankind's liberation through faith—not violent rebellion—from the thrall of bondage to the Devil.

And there is a true freedom, found only in the service of God and man, done according to the divine Law which Israel received as soon as it was out of Egypt.

Christianity, unlike ideology, proclaims liberation *from* to guarantee freedom *for,* and defines both! We will examine how in our concluding section.

PART **III**

What Is Liberation Theology?

In the first place, liberation *expresses the aspirations of oppressed peoples and classes, emphasizing the conflictual aspect of the economic, social, and political process which puts them at odds with wealthy nations and oppressive classes.*

Gustavo Gutierrez

At a deeper level, liberation *can be applied to an understanding of history. Man is seen as assuming conscious responsiblity for his own destiny.*

Gustavo Gutierrez

The word liberation *allows for another approach leading to the Biblical sources which inspire the presence and action of man in history.*

Gustavo Gutierrez

These latest theologies agree in projecting a theology that is practical, public, and critical. In this context theology is defined or redefined as "critical reflection in and on historical praxis." The key to this shift of theology towards praxis can be found in Marx's eleventh thesis on Feuerbach.

Alfredo Fierro

6

Liberation Theology Defined

For definition of Liberation Theology we turn to what is commonly cited as the "classic" exposition of it, *A Theology Of Liberation* by Peruvian Catholic priest Gustavo Gutierrez.

Published in Spanish in 1971, in Lima, Peru, Gutierrez' volume was Englished by Sister Caridad Inda and John Eagleson and published by Orbis Books of Maryknoll, New York, in 1973 (43).

We have already alluded to the question whether there is sufficient consensus among Liberationists to permit defining Liberation Theology as one entity. The intent of such a query, we have also suggested, is to blunt criticism by diffusing its impact.

Such a question is often posed concerning Marxism, formulated like this: is there not so wide a difference among Marxists and Marxist parties in the world as to prohibit their common identification as "Marxism?"

It is obvious that such a query has the force of an affirmation, namely that because of the diversity of views on specifics, no critique of Marxism really hits the mark as concerns any particular theorist, party or nation. Neat if it deflects the critic or confuses the reader.

Such may also be the intent of those who stress the diversity among Theologians of Liberation.

But the issue in fact, rather than in rhetoric, as regards both Marxism and LT, is simple enough: does the term "Marxism" or the term "Liberation Theology" have reference to a reality or to a myth? If there is a reality denoted by the term "Marxism" and one denoted by the term "Liberation Theology"—and most certainly there is!—then any deviant species share enough of the genus to be called Marxism or LT. And it is about that central core of meaning that discussion can proceed.

Let those who try to use the supposed diversities among Liberation Theologians to defuse critique show that these Theologians do in fact point out in each other the Marxist-mandated defects we will be discussing below. Until this is done, we will claim that LT displays a common cause and essence which define it more than clearly enough for discussion.

The reader who peruses LT publications will not find one Liberationist explicitly denying the name to another, while all commonly speak of "we" and "our" and the like.

It will be accurate enough, then, to derive a definition of Liberation Theology from the "classic" author Gutierrez, and to discuss LT in terms of what he says it is, deriving additional insight from other writers as we go along.

"Theology," Gutierrez writes, "must be man's critical reflection on himself, on his own basic principles. Only with this approach will theology be a serious discourse, aware of itself, in full possession of its conceptual elements. . . . We also refer to a clear and critical attitude regarding economic and socio-cultural issues in the life and reflection of the Christian community."

Again: "Theology is reflection, a critical attitude. Theology *follows;* it is the second step. . . . Theology does not produce pastoral activity; rather it reflects upon it."

Further: "A theology which has as its points of reference only 'truths' which have been established once and for all—and not the Truth which is also the Way—can only be static and, in the long run, sterile."

And: "Theology as critical reflection on historical praxis is a liberating theology. . . . This is a theology which does not stop with reflecting on the world, but rather tries to be part of the process through which the world is transformed" (43:11-15).

Earlier Gutierrez has written: ". . . we pay special attention in this work to the critical function of theology with respect to the presence and activity of man in history. . . . the struggle to construct a just and fraternal society, where people can live with dignity and be the agents of their own destiny. . . . *Liberation* . . . emphasizes that man transforms himself by conquering his liberty throughout his existence and his history" (46:x).

If the reader is puzzled by the precise meaning of the term "reflection," as Liberationists use it, he will after some exposure to this Theology decide that by "reflection" the Liberationist means whatever thoughts are coursing through his head at the moment. Presumably they may be dubbed "theological" because the head belongs to a theologian.

If the reader already detects Marxist overtones in Gutierrez' definition of Liberation Theology, he will hear these becoming louder to the point of drowning out the voice of the Bible before we are through.

And if the reader wonders why LT ignores the etymological meaning of "theology" as "the science" (*logy*) of "God (*theos*), he has missed a hint already suggested by Gutierrez: to rest theology only (!) on "truths that have been established once and for all"—like the Bible—is to render it a "sterile" thing! We will hear more of such rejection of divine revelation as we listen further to Gutierrez and colleagues.

Brazilian Liberationist Hugo Assmann adds the following to a definition of LT: "The theology of liberation takes a decisive step in the direction of the secular sciences by admitting that the fact of human experience, on which the secular sciences have the first word to say, is its basic point of reference, its contextual starting-point" (5:62-63). That Marxism is the first of those "secular sciences" which get the "first word" in LT will soon become clear.

For now: Liberation Theology is critical reflection upon man in the process of achieving his own liberation, done from within the revolutionary milieu and contributing to it.

By this definition, Marx and Engels would no doubt fit into the category of "theologians," and Marxism, to their surprise if not chagrin, could be baptized as "theological reflection!"

7

Liberation Theology and Marxism

What is the relation between Marxism and LT?

It is this:

Marxism has written the script which LT recites as if it were its very own dramatic discovery!

To demonstrate that, we begin by noting that LT makes no secret of its alliance with Marxism, and that in two ways:

1) LT boldly chooses to use Marxism as a tool for social analysis, on the risky assumption that one can give the finger to ideology and not lose the whole hand.

2) LT goes even further to pronounce an essential unity between Marxism and what it understands by Christianity.

1. Marxism As a Tool

Gutierrez writes: "Pointing the way towards an era in history when man can live humanly, Marx created categories which allowed for the elaboration of a science of history" (43:30). These, as we have just noticed above, become the context for LT's theological reflection.

The Marxists were, writes George Mueller in his Foreword to Joseph Petulla's *Christian Political Theology,* a "people who were more committed to radical social and political change than were traditional Christians . . . action that is relevant only when the issues have been exposed to a forceful Marxian analysis" (74:viii). This explains, Mueller says, why Petulla subtitles his book "A Marxian Guide."

Petulla himself argues that a political theology (the term preferred in Europe for LT) develops a methodology "which requires an analytical instrument for grappling with the social processes of the world. Marxism provides such a powerful analytical tool" (74:2). Petulla writes out of the USA, but does "theological reflection" in tandem with Latin American Liberationists. "The reason that this book is presented as a

'Marxian Guide' to political theology," he explains, "is that we have accepted a Marxian methodology in our model of societal analysis" (74:28).

Hugo Assmann reports of Latin American Liberation Theologians, "In general they realize that the traditional contributions of Christian social teaching—which has been discussed with growing freedom in Latin America in recent years—are wholly inadequate for acting on the more radical implications of the faith as the practice of liberation. As a result, until a viable Christian body of thought can be elaborated, they inevitably turn to the analytical techniques of Marxism, often without taking account of the possible overall consequences" (5:138). What Assmann means, of course, is that in LT's opinion no body of "Christian social teaching" can be considered "viable" until taken over by Marxism. What he fails to appreciate is that when this happens, as it does in LT, that social thought is no longer Christian! Just how radically viable a genuinely Christian social doctrine and action can be will be illustrated in the final section of this book.

Writing in a collection of essays by Liberation Theolgians, Gutierrez insists, "Only a class-based [that is Marxist] analysis will enable us to see what is really involved in the opposition between oppressed countries on the one hand and dominant peoples on the other" (39:17). LT uses Marxism to impose the "class struggle" slogan upon international as well as upon internal relations.

Peruvian Catholic Liberationist Raul Vidales asserts, "Liberation theology presupposes the voice of the human sciences, of the social sciences in particular, as its first or preliminary theological word. . . . The basic contribution of the human sciences is to provide theology with a more clear-eyed view of history, a more critical approach, and a set of analytical instruments" (39:41).

First among those "human sciences" which provide LT with its "first . . . theological word" is of course Marxism, which its founders were very careful to describe as a genuinely "scientific" approach to human relationships. Liberation Theologians are fond of the "scientific" character of Marxism—perhaps because it serves their purposes in seeming to demean, by comparison, the Bible's—presumably unscientific—analyses of human behavior.

We recognize that some Liberationists like Columbian Catholic Segundo Galilea try to minimize LT's use of Marx. He holds that it is but "one current of the 'ideologized' liberation theology [that] tends to rely on Marxist categories for its interpretation of liberation, dependence, politics, and liberative commitment."

Note that Galilea does perceive Marxism as an ideology, but his contention is that though the Marxist "current" in LT "is a rather limited one, it leads some people to suspect liberation theology as a whole. They fear that it has been infiltrated by Marxism and that it leads to 'horizontalism,' pure politicism, and a merely temporal humanism" (43:170). How well founded this "fear" really is will emerge as we go along.

Galilea admonishes LT critics: "Needless to say, it is quite unfair to extend that criticism to liberation theology as a whole. No serious theologian in Latin America who is truly representative of our current Christian thinking goes along with that approach" (39:170).

He is right on one thing: it would be unfair to tar LT with a Marxist brush. But on Galilea's ground, either the theologians studied in the following pages fail of being fully "serious," or his attempted exoneration is far wide of the truth. The reader can, however, both from our quotations and by reference to the sources we will carefully indicate, decide for himself whether many Liberationist's views turn out to have been not only "infiltrated by Marxism" but in fact pipe to Marx's tune.

Alfredo Fierro, Catholic Liberationist writing out of Madrid, provides an unintentional commentary on Galilea's contention that the number of Liberation Theologians who employ Marxist categories is small by writing: "Many of today's theologians, and almost all those who have concerned themselves with political theology, seem to admit unreservedly the validity of the Marxist analysis insofar as socioeconomic realities are concerned. Current political theology takes for an accepted fact the historical-materialist interpretation of production relationships, social classes, political power, and the social processes of change" (33:114).

He goes on to quote Liberationist José Comblin as saying that ours "is the era of Marx," and German political-theologian Nell-Breuning as "admitting" that "all of us are standing on Marx's shoulders" (33:366). This last is a contention frequently emphasized by French Marxist Jean Paul Sartre. No one, Sartre was fond of saying, can henceforth do social analysis without taking appreciative account of the thought of Marx. He might, it appears, so far as LT is concerned, have said that no one can henceforth do theology without "first" attending to the word out of *Capital!*

The thrust of Liberation Theology, despite Galilea's demurrer, is obviously a deliberate orientation toward Marxism. It would be "unfair" not to point that out!

Thus it is already obvious that, for Liberation Theology, Marx guards the gate through which LT's "theological reflection" enters the arena of human life.

2. Marxism and Christianity As Equivalents

There are Liberation Theologians who not only find Marxism an indispensable tool to understanding society but who also find in Marxism the key to what God is up to in history. These theologians do not hesitate to pronounce an essential identity between Marxism and Christianity.

Consider the subtle and sustained effort to draw out the presumed identity in Catholic Mexican José Miranda's *Marx And The Bible*.

"The God of the Bible," Miranda says, "has a plan; he has resolved to change our world into a world of justice." And to whom has God revealed that plan?

Let Miranda tell us: "In history, within history, there is an *eschaton*, an *ultimum*, toward which all the partial realizations of justice are directed. Here I must point out that this *ultimum*, this *novum*, also characterizes the philosophy of Marx" (66:87).

At least for this Liberation Theologian, Christianity and Marxism are running, not on parallel tracks but on the same one.

Miranda is also certain that he perceives a unity between Marx and the Bible, which has hitherto escaped others: "Between faith and dialectical thinking," he says, "there is a common denominator considerably more serious than Western positivistic scientists disparagingly are accustomed to believe. . . ." The "dialectical thinking" which he has in mind, Miranda says, is that "of Hegel and Marx." There are, he adds, "so many convergences" between Marxist thought and the Christian faith that "there must be an underlying profound affinity which has not yet be brought completely to light" (66:201).

It is an "affinity" which Miranda undertakes to reveal: "The first and decisive affinity is that Marx believes that dialectics will produce justice in the world, and the Bible believes that faith will produce justice in the world—real justice, not fictitious justice, not a merely imputed justice as the Protestants of old sustained" (66:202). What "underlying profound affinity" there is between "dialectics" and "faith" is unclear, being as they are quite separate routes to "justice."

Another "affinity:" "Marx is on the same side as the biblical authors: he does believe that there is hope for our world" (66:217).

And another: "Marx and Paul coincide in their intuition of the totality of evil. Sin and injustice form an all-comprehensive and all-pervasive organic structure. Paul calls this totality *kosmos*. Marx calls it 'capitalism' " (66:250)—and Miranda calls it an *identity!*

Perhaps it is not surprising that "affinities" of such tenuous relationship have evaded discovery.

But Miranda pursues the theme: "Both for the Bible and for Marx selfishness and the State are precisely 'fallen' facts, not natural ones. Precisely for this reason we believe that man can cease being selfish and merciless and self-serving and can find his greatest fulness in loving his neighbor" (66:255).

Miranda persists: "Above we saw that in both Marx and the Bible the basis for all thought is this thesis which is the most revolutionary imaginable: Sin and evil are not inherent to humanity and history; they began one day through human work and they can, therefore, be eliminated" (66:277).

Without comment on the absurdity of imposing an "underlying profound affinity" in the reckless parallels Miranda imagines, the point we are stressing comes clear: this Liberationist is bent upon establishing, and claiming it a new discovery, an "identity" between his Marxism and the Bible. One thing that does become obvious all through Miranda's belabored attempt at forging his "synthesis" of Marxism and the Bible is this: Marx plays the tune to which the Bible whistles (when permitted) the obbligato. Marx lights the way, and benighted old Paul, like the rest of the Scripture, trails obediently after. Marxism and the Bible are siblings of one stock, as Miranda misrepresents the case, with the Bible the older but Marx the wiser brother.

Alfredo Fierro attempts to forge an alliance between Marxism and theology in terms of "praxis" (that is, action): "The key to this shift of theology towards praxis can be found in Marx's eleventh thesis against Feuerbach: 'Philosophers have done nothing more than *interpret* the world in different ways; but it is really a matter of *transforming* it' " (33:22-23). Therefore, he says, "Political theology is a theology operating under the sign of Marx, just as truly as scholasticism was a theology operating under the sign of Aristotle and liberal Protestant theology was one operating under the sign of Kant" (33:80). Indeed, Fierro holds, "Political theology is the specific and proper form of theology in an epoch dominated by Marx" (33:102).

Liberationist Paul Blanquart is quoted to the effect that the believer "is not a revolutionary because he is a Christian; rather, being a revolutionary is his way of being a Christian" (33:150). Fierro adds that Blanquart is able to draw out three parallels between Christianity and Marxism—on the level of rationality, on that of seeking the "whole person," and on that of a motivating ideology (33: 243-44). Christianity and Marxism are, as it were, twins from the same revolutionary stock.

With a refreshing frankness, Fierro makes no secret of his priorities: "To put it succinctly, we shall adopt Marxism as our hypothesis and then go on to consider what sort of theology is possible on that basis." Note that he is not arguing for the use of Marxism as a tool, but as a foundation. He goes on to say what this order of precedence implies:

"More and more people are saying: 'I profess to be a Christian, but I declare myself a Marxist' "—the quotation being taken from a Latin American, Luis N. Rivera Pagan (33:371).

This remark does bring to light the hierarchy of authority in this unity which Liberationist ideology forces between Marxism and theology: first, Marx; then, such scattered fragments of the Bible as can be adapted to Marxist mandates. First the declaration of allegiance (to Marxism), and then the profession of faith (in the God of the Scriptures)!

In summary, LT begins with using Marxism as an analytical tool, and finds itself discovering, with as little surprise as regret, a hitherto unnoticed identity between Marxism and Christianity.

Joseph Petulla affirms both of these relations as follows: "In this essay we are affirming, among other things, that Marxism and Christianity share a basic symbolic 'onlook' and because they hold this 'onlook' in common, Christian political theology may utilize a method derived from Marxian critical theory" (74:21).

Petulla adds that "A comparison of Marxian and Christian onlooks towards liberation again shows striking similarities. Both traditions base their theories of liberation on the concept of community" (74:164).

In practice it turns out that Christian political theology does not "utilize" Marxism, but quite the other way around. It is Marxism that sends Liberationist "theological reflection" upon its errands in the wilderness of speculation. And it is ideology which enslaves such theology as LT squeezes selectively out of the Bible. The analytical tool has taken over the analyst!

3. Summary

It will become increasingly transparent, as we go along, that the Liberationist starts from a Marxist commitment, and then derives from the Bible, and reads into Christianity, whatever suits his allegiance to Marxism.

But how could it be otherwise?

Ideology serves only the ideologue, and acknowledges no equals. It knows only competitors whom it intends to dominate or destroy.

Fascism is like Marxism a bloodthirsty ideology. A line taken from one of the last letters written by Count (Graf) Helmuth von Moltke to his wife before his execution as an enemy of Hitler's Third Reich illustrates the determination of an ideology to rule or kill. Von Moltke cites an aphorism shouted at him by Nazi hangman-Judge Rudolf Freisler, who condemned him to death: "Herr Graf, we National Socialists and Christianity have one thing in common, and only one: we demand the whole of a man!" (40:231). But Christianity, as we shall see, claims the believer for freedom, while the ideology binds its victims body and soul.

Christianity *or* ideology, the word of the Lord *or* the word of the ideologue. Nothing makes this mutual exclusion clearer than the dominant role which Marx comes to play in every effort to make "Christian" use of Marxist categories or to equate Christian and Marxist "onlooks."

8

The Four Pillars of Liberation Theology

To show precisely how Marxism has taken over Liberation Theology, let us recall the four pillars of Marxism and indicate their status in Liberation Theology. We will find that LT overtly subordinates itself to these Marxist categories, not simply as lenses through which to view the world but as constituents of its own "theology."

1. Liberation Theology Adopts the Class Struggle Analysis (Marxism 1)

The first pillar of Marxism is the slogan of "class struggle."

LT adopts the same slogan.

Gustavo Gutierrez is very sure: "The class struggle is a fact and neutrality in this question is not possible" (43:275).

LT is commonly very exclusive: ". . . neutrality in this question is not possible!"

Enzo Gatti, Catholic priest writing from Italy, implies that class struggle reveals the will of Christ: "It is his limitless love for man that makes Christ divide the world into halves—or, rather, makes him reduce all the oppressive divisions which man introduces into the world to a single division: the division between those who suffer and those who cause suffering."

"Precisely because Christ is so concerned," Gatti adds, "with the destinies of men—with man's salvation and full humanization, his freedom and dignity—he had to make preferential choices, that is, to take the side of the weak against the strong, the oppressed against the oppressor" (37:41-42). Gatti's Christ not only reduces social tensions to Marxist dimensions, but participates in the class struggle.

First joint Marxist-LT pillar, then: all society is warped by class struggle.

2. Liberation Theology Condemns Private Property (Marxism 2)

Marxism posits the private ownership of the means of production as the root of class struggle. Marxism therefore demands the abolition of the right to such private ownership.

So does Liberation Theology.

LT even tries to equate private-ownership capitalism with the biblical notion of "sin."

We will divide this section into two parts, then: a) LT accepts the Marxist lead in tracing class struggle to the private ownership of the means of production; b) to do so, LT equates capitalism with "sin."

a) LT Traces Class Struggle To Private Ownership

José Miranda opens his treatise with "the attack of this book against the right of ownership. . . ." In a few sentences he is discoursing on "the injustice of ownership . . ." and equating private ownership of productive means, as Marx does, with "robbery" (66:2-3). Soon he is suborning the Bible to Marx's analysis: "The fact that differentiating [privately owned] wealth is unacquirable without violence and spoliation is presupposed by the Bible . . ." (66:19).

"Presupposed by the Bible"? Indeed? Where? Were not Zacchaeus, singled out for favor by Jesus Himself, and Joseph of Arimathaea, acquaintance of Pilate and disciple of Jesus, and Matthew, disciple and tax collector, as well as the Patriarchs of Israel all rich? And does not the Bible attribute wealth to God's blessing? The Spirit teaches through the Prophet Samuel: "The Lord makes poor and makes rich; he brings low, he also exalts" (I Sam. 2:7).

LT joins Marxism in denouncing capitalism and the private ownership of the means of production:

"Capitalism is not merely an economic technique . . . but the result of the will to exploit, of a strategy of exploitation, of oppressing violence, and of a structure of mechanisms of exploitation," says José María Diez-Alegría, Catholic Liberationist writing from Rome, in his *I Believe In Hope*. "For this realization," he adds, "I am indebted to Karl Marx" (23:44).

Describing Liberationists as "dissident Christians," Dennis Goulet reports in his *A New Moral Order*, "These new and vocal Christians favor liberation over law and order, and they plead for broad participation of the masses in taking decisions and actions for change, as opposed to elitist or top-down models of planning. They reject capitalism—even a capitalism which is rectified or attenuated by welfare policies—as radically immoral and structurally incompatible with social justice" (41:83). We cannot but observe that were these "dissident Christians" half as sensitive to morality and justice as they profess to be, their first condemnation would be of the totalitarian states, where social immorality and legalized injustice are institutionalized.

A Protestant Liberationist, Jos Miguez Bonino, writing out of Argentina, tells us, "For us Latin Americans today socialism, as a socio-economic structure and a historical project, is viewed as our active correlation with the presence of the kingdom insofar as the structure of human society is concerned. On that level it represents our obedience in faith and it is the matrix of theological reflection" (39:278).

In the future which LT envisions: "Private ownership of the means of production will be eliminated because it enables a few to expropriate the fruits of labor performed by the many, generates class divisions in society, and permits one class to be exploited by another" (43:1-2). Thus Gustavo Gutierrez, in obvious obedience to the dictates of Marx.

So far we note that LT opts for the Marxist denunciation of private ownership of productive property.

In an effort to fit "theological" attire to its Marxist analysis, LT finds it convenient to equate capitalism with "sin." How this is attempted is worth the observing.

b) Capitalism As "Sin"

The Bible condemns "sin."

The "theological" value, therefore, of focusing the biblical condemnation of "sin" on the socio-economic structures one wishes to destroy is obvious. LT quite naturally, therefore, tries to equate capitalism with "sinful structures."

"The root of social injustice," Gutierrez tells us, "is sin" (43:21). No Christian disagrees, until he realizes that for Gutierrez & Company that "root of social injustice" is private property and the capitalist system which rests upon it: "For sinfulness occurs in the negation of human beings as brothers and sisters, in oppressive structures created for the benefit of only a few, and in the plundering of nations, races, cultures, and social classes" (43:21)—all the code words for condemning capitalism.

Segundo Galilea has it this way: "Liberation theology is rooted in three assumptions that form the Christian's view of the present juncture in Latin American history: (1) The present situation is one in which the vast majority of Latin Americans live in a state of underdevelopment and unjust dependence; (2) viewed in Christian terms, this is a 'sinful situation'; (3) hence it is the duty of Christians in conscience, and of the church in its pastoral activity, to commit themselves to efforts to overcome this situation" (39:167). The reader need be but moderately sensitive to what is being said between the lines to find here the baptism of a Marxist analysis of private ownership of productive means as key to a "sinful situation." This becomes clear as Galilea procedes:

"In liberation terms sinners are the exploiters and those who act unjustly" (39:169). In short, "sinners" are the bourgeoisie.

Enrique Dussel, Catholic Liberationist layman writing out of Argentina, expresses his view succinctly: "Sin is nothing else but the domination of the 'other.' Political sinfulness is nothing else but the domination and alienation of one's fellow human being and brother, of the 'other' embodied in a colonized country, an oppressed class, an impoverished people . . . Salvation (or redemption) means liberation from that oppression" (39:208).

Hugo Assmann, Brazilian Catholic theologian, thinks of "sin" as "institutionalized violence" (5:67), and thinks of "institutionalized violence" as characteristic of capitalist societies. Liberationists of many hues are fond of caricaturing the *status quo* in the democracies as one of "institutionalized violence"—a term they do not use concerning the Communist states, where if anywhere, violence and the threat of violence are "institutionalized!"

Note on "Institutionalized Violence"

But what is "institutionalized violence?"

It's simply another slogan which neatly serves ideological purposes. It is designed to stimulate a spirit of rebellion against established order. The deception lies in suggesting that the authority which must structure any form of society functions as "institutionalized violence."

The trick is to justify violence against social order by portraying that order as itself actively violent. It's easy, once you get the hang of it:

Look twice at the social institutions which make society possible—like schools, homes, businesses, the state, etc. Being institutions, they will have patterns of order and rules of conduct.

And if there are rules, then there must be some kind of penalty upon violation of the rules. Ah, but can't you see that this implies *violence?*

Is there discipline in the classrooms? But that's violence with a smiling face! Is there structure in industry? are there rules in the work place? must the job be begun on time? How simple to label them all as but varieties of "institutionalized violence!"

And must the police deal with lawlessness, and the courts judge the criminal? You can, with a little dose of ideology, perceive that all this is but "violent" abuse of people's rights.

Even discipline in the home can be construed as the iron fist in the velvet glove of parental "love"—violence on the sly!

It's a slogan, for there is not a word in LT publications about "institutionalized violence" in the very societies that reek of it most, that is the cold, gray totalitarianism of the Communist states.

Beware, then, of that wily slogan "institutionalized violence"—those who use it have designs that will impose it upon you!

In sum, LT not only joins Marxism in condemning the private ownership of the means of productive property, but tries to bring such ownership under the biblical denunciation of "sin!" Something of an achievement in would-be deception!

Note on Sin and Evil

We append a note on LT's crucial confusion of "sin" with "evil."

The Bible often uses the terms "sin" and "evil" interchangably. So do we all. But there is, in the Scriptures, a fundamental discrimination between them, which LT, like Marxism, does not acknowledge.

Strictly speaking, man *sins* against God—in violation of the First Table of the Law: "You shall love the Lord your God with all your heart, and with all your soul, and with all your mind. This is the great and first commandment" (Matt. 22:37-38).

And, strictly speaking, man compounds sin by doing *evil* against his neighbor—in violation of the Second Table of the Law: "And a second is like it, You shall love your neighbor as yourself. On these two commandments depend all the law and the prophets" (Matt. 22:39-40). We can "sin" only against the will of God; we do "evil" against what is God's, namely ourselves, our neighbors and God's creation.

Sin is the root of evil, and all evil-doing involves sin. But sin itself is disobedience to God. Sin is, therefore, vertical misdoing; evil is horizontal.

Both Marxism and LT pay no mind to this crucial distinction, both thinking only on the horizontal level of human relations, characterized by evil. And this is why both ideologies sanguinely assume that man can, if he puts his will to it, cure his propensity to misdoing.

St. Paul writes: "The saying is sure and worthy of full acceptance, that Christ Jesus came into the world to save sinners" (I Tim. 1:15).

And who, in Liberation Theology are those "sinners?"

The bourgeoisie!

They are the "sinners," while the proletariat are the "sinned against!"

On this basis, the Christ who, according to the Bible, came to save sinners, would have come only for the bourgeoisie! Far from infusing the "sinned against" with rebellious fire, Jesus would have come to rescue their oppressors! How flat a contradiction to the LT determination to find in the Bible the fuel for violent uprising by the sinned-against against the sinners!

The LT error lies in its failure to discriminate "sin" from "evil." But LT makes this error so that it can, like Marx, anticipate man's own self-redemption. If LT were to acknowledge that "sin" is done against God, and evil against one's fellows, then only God—not man—can forgive sin. This fact implies the whole biblical soteriology, the gift by God of His Son to atone for sin—an atonement man cannot make, but only receive through faith, not wrest from God's hand via rebellion!

Psalm 51 vividly illumines the distinction we are here stressing between sin and evil. The Psalm gives voice to David's profound contrition over his adultery with Bathsheba and his contrived murder of her husband Uriah (cf. 2 Samuel 11-13). What does David say?

He cries out to God, "Against thee, thee only, have I sinned, and done that which is evil in thy sight"(Ps. 51:4).

What the penitent king confesses to Him from whom no secrets are hid is a double contrition: against God he has sinned, and against the others done evil. But the evil, too, is noted by God because abused Bathsheba and her murdered husband also are His!

But is it only against God that David *sinned?*

Yes, only against God.

Sin is ever and only against God, committed whenever and wherever man takes himself, or another, or an ideology, or a fad as normative for behavior! Sin is defined in the First Table of the divine Law, beginning with the first commandment: "You shall have no other gods before me!" (Ex. 20:3; Deut. 5:7).

There is no way, except through confession and contrition like David's, acceptable because the Son of God expiates the guilt, that man can atone for his sins. A biblical certainty which Marx avoids by rejecting the Bible and LT detours by confusing sin and evil.

Marx and LT hope to eliminate man's evil to man through rebellion, but the root of human evil-doing is not class struggle or private ownership. It is sin! And this is why the totalitarian Marxist state does not mitigate evil, neither in quantity nor variety—it is based on the sin of ideology, the idol of the rebellious!

It was "sin," and not evil, that brought Adam and Eve down in the Garden. It is a heritage of that sin which now taints all of the human race, a taint only cleansed in the blood of Christ shed on Calvary, never in the blood however copiously spilled in the throes of rebellion.

Second Marxist-LT pillar, then: class struggle roots in the legal right to private ownership of the means of production.

3. Liberation Theology Endorses Violent Rebellion (Marxism 3)

"In short," writes Petulla, "the work of political theology is social change, and in the long run, radical social change" (74:31).

"In the framework of the Latin American political context . . . we must recognize the fact that there is conflict between various social classes, that we do have class enemies, and that those enemies must be combatted" (43:11-12)—so says Gutierrez. "It comes down," in his view, "to taking a socialist and revolutionary stand" (39:9). And, with the usual absolutism: "Only by getting beyond a society divided into classes, only by establishing a form of political power designed to serve the vast majority of our people, and only by eliminating private ownership of the wealth created by human labor will we be able to lay the foundations for a more just society" (39:17-18).

The Liberation Theologian does not parallel Marxism; he simply parrots it!

But where has Marxism in praxis, after more than half a century of experiment, produced any but the very antithesis of "a more just society?" There is, unhappily, little that an ideology more readily avoids than the test of precisely that "praxis" which LT is forever pretending to take seriously.

Luis del Valle, writing from Mexico City, enlists the Church in Marxist rebellion: "A practical ecclesiology of this sort assumes at the start that the church will seek to serve the poor. Its service will not be apolitical; it will seek to help those who are oppressed by structures to fight for their own liberation" (39:89).

The Liberationist seems oblivious to the irony of *his* urging the Church to provide the poor with bullets rather than bread, for that is the criticism commonly levelled against the bourgeoisie.

Third Marxist-LT pillar, then: overthrow of the capitalist system through violent proletarian rebellion.

4. For Liberation Theology the "New Man" Redeems Himself (Marxism 4)

We may remind ourselves that, in the words of Harvard Professor Adam B. Ulam, it was Marx's view "that the emancipation of the working class must be the deed of the working class itself" (147). History, for Marx, provided the resources for its own redemption—a view which required Marx (and requires LT) to ignore the Fall of man.

We return, here, to the crux of revolutionary Marxism, and, no less, of Liberation Theology: man *can* remake himself! Through violent rebellion! It is in the uncertain light of this immense assumption that, as we have seen, ideology justifies all manner of evil!

Does the Liberationist not even sense the absurdity of a creature so desperately in need of redemption as man repeatedly demonstrates himself to be, undertaking to redeem himself? Like assigning a lost traveler to drawing his own map to where he wants to go! Indeed, unperceived by liberal humanisms of all kinds is man's inability to diagnose on his own the nature of the malady which subtly corrupts, sometimes more and sometimes less conspicuously, his every social relationship.

The savage irony of all this is ignored by ideologues who silence when they can all criticism and destroy when they are able all who dare to differ aloud.

"For Marx," writes Petulla, "man defines himself by creative praxis. Man is a producing artist. . . . men realize themselves in and through nature. Man creates the world, transforms nature, makes his own civilization" (74:35). And in the process re-news himself!

Revolutionary Che Guevara posits a "vanguard" of those who see the contours of both present and future in the light of Marxist categories. Che says, "The vanguard has its eyes fixed on the future and its rewards, but this is not seen as something personal. The reward is a new society in which men will have attained new features: the society of communist man" (74:146-47).

Out of the ashes of the violent revolt he advocated, Che beholds the rise of a "new" man creating a "new" society—essentially a belief that Hegel was correct: out of "negation" will come affirmation, a miracle which has yet to be realized. "We will," Guevara adds, "forge ourselves in daily action, creating a new man with a new technology" (74:150). LT and Marxism are in accord: man will redeem himself!

We have already heard José Miranda say, "Both for the Bible and for Marx selfishness and the State are precisely 'fallen' facts, not natural ones. Precisely for this reason we believe that man can cease being selfish and merciless and self-serving and can find his greatest fulness in loving his neighbor. We reject the imposition of an allegedly unchangeable nature, in virtue of which man will be a wolf to man as long as there is history . . . If the West calls Marx utopian, it must first give up its pretense and call the Gospel utopian" (66:255).

But the Gospel never posits man as perfected this side of eternity.

There is no "pretense" about the Bible's clear-eyed realism: the wheat of the Kingdom and the tares of the Adversary grow together, and even in the soul of man en route to redemption through faith sunshine and shadow grapple (cf. Romans 7).

What Miranda means, anyhow, is that for Marx and for the Bible (*as LT expurgates it*) the view of man as capable of self-redemption is the same.

Alfredo Fierro: "Only present-day theology can and does operate on the premise that people are conscious and critical subjects of history . . . revolution being nothing but the creation of human beings by and for themselves" (33:29). The Marxist master's voice in theological syllables!

But, the "new" man created in the crucible of violence is so far something of a disaster. So much so, that the unhappy, enslaved peoples being made "new" under the vanguard of the proletariat never get the chance to register by secret ballot what they think of the process of their self-creation!

This plain lesson of history is, however, lost on the LT ideologist, as Fierro goes on to demonstrate: "Is it 'new' people who create a new society or is it the new society that will produce new people?"

It is a decisive question, one we have already discussed. How opportune a juncture for a Liberationist to take a long, hard look at the tyrants which Marxist ideology has loosed upon mankind—challenging the Marxist assumption that changed social relationships create new men. It hasn't worked that way! But, self-blinded to that, our LT ideologist falls into his own ditch:

We repeat: "The older moralism naively believed that the conversion of human individuals would be enough. [We wonder whose naive "moralism" he has in view; not Augustine's, surely, nor Aquinas' or Calvin's.] Indeed it may have even felt that structural changes and reforms were useless." Note: ". . . may even have felt"—is this history or fantasy?

Fierro fares on: "Persuaded by the evidence gathered by social theory [no doubt he means Marxism], current theology knows that there can be no transformation of human beings without the transformation of society. In the last analysis, societal transformation comes down to a transformation of production relationships. Real conversion to a new humanity must necessarily go by way of revolution" (33:235-36).

Assmann introduces a quotation from Gutierrez as follows: "The only Christological meaning of creation and salvation (Col. 1: 15-20) is summed up in the phrase 'creation of a new man,' which is so close to the spirit of many revolutionary writings today: 'When we state that man realizes his potential in prolonging the work of creation through his labour, we mean that by virtue of this fact he places himself inside the process of saving history. Building the earthly city is not a simple state of "humanization," or "pre-evangelization," as the theology of a few years ago used to have it; it is integrating oneself fully in a saving process that embraces all mankind' " (5:67-68). There will be occasion below to consider what LT means by "salvation." What matters here is that with one voice Liberation Theologians adopt the Marxist theory that man can renovate himself.

Paulo Freire, Latin American educationist, writes in his Foreword to Dennis Goulet's *A New Moral Order:* "Authentic prophecy cannot be achieved in the absence of a dialectic unity between denunciation of the oppressive reality and annunciation of a new reality, which will give birth to a new man and a new woman" (41:xiii).

An "annunciation" of a "new reality"—a truly *new* reality!—does put the faithful in mind of an event celebrated in painting and liturgy when indeed the intrusion of something "new" into history was announced: Gabriel's announcement to Mary that she would "give birth" to a Son who "will be called holy, the Son of God" (Luke 1:26-38). In Him, indeed, is the promise of men and women becoming "new" under the discipline of faith, and of an eternal kingdom proleptically theirs! But Freire is not thinking of the meaning of Christmas; his mind is on what mankind will do for itself:

"This merger of denouncing with announcing is what establishes the revolutionary praxis of the dominated classes in union with their leaders" (37:xiii). The phrase, "with their leaders" will alert the perceptive to what Marx called, and Lenin was to create as "the dictatorship of the proletariat." Revolutionary praxis has, indeed, announced and effected the birth of that monstrous creation, one which shows no signs of fulfilling Lenin's prediction of withering away.

José Comblin asserts, "The effect of true Christian preaching is precisely the appearance of a people as a new reality different from the state. Such a new, free unit does not come from any power above the human beings who create it. A people comes from human beings and nothing else" (18:194). Comblin leaves no room for alternatives: *only* man remakes man!

Fourth Marxist-LT pillar, then: man will make himself "new" through rebellion and its consequent classless society.

5. Summary: The Four Basic Pillars of Marxism/Liberation Theology

We have now observed that the four basic pillars of Marxism also structure Liberation Theology. Briefly:

1. The root of human evil lies in class struggle.
2. The root of class struggle lies in the private ownership of the means of production.
3. Only violent revolution will destroy such private ownership.
4. Out of such revolution, and through it, man will make himself "new."

The crucial consensus, then, upon which both LT and Marxism converge is this: mankind has within itself the resources for complete self-renovation. Man is his own savior!

Tweedle-dum and Tweedle-dee! But for LT Marx comes first, and LT chooses to disciple itself, not to the Christ of the Bible, but to the ideology of Marx!

What is evident to the outside observer is that Marxism, in this relationship, is the *exploiter* and LT the *exploited!*

The Liberation Theologian's most decisive act of "liberation" would be breaking free from his Marxist shackles! But this would, in fact, leave LT with nothing to parade as "new," and little to call its own.

9

Profile of Liberation Theology

We deal in this chapter with the ambience, the environment, which LT creates for itself. Liberation Theology displays a certain psychological or spiritual profile which reveals a good deal about the mood in which its "theological reflection" is pursued.

We highlight some facets of that profile here.

1. Exclusively Ours!

Though LT is heavily dependent upon Marxism, it claims to recognize no equals, especially among other theologians and theologies. In this respect it apes Marx who notoriously brooked no criticism and recognized no equals, even destroying the First International Working Men's Association when he feared losing control of it.

But before counting exclusivism a defect, the reader will perhaps reflect that Christianity also seems to be exclusivist: "No one comes to the Father, but by me," as Jesus, for example, says (John 14:6).

Is it not, then, as natural to theology as to ideology to be adamantly exclusivist? And are not our occasional references to LT's constant "our way or none" simply as true of orthodox Christianity?

No, the parallel is inexact.

God, and the Christ brook no equals. True.

But no Christian theology claims for itself a monopoly upon the Truth to the exclusion of all others. None, that is, except LT!

All authentic Christian theology, recognizing itself as human construct, invites or implies comparison with its infallible reference, the Bible. Luther before the Diet of Worms, for example, with his life in the balance, did not claim license from the Spirit or his own unique praxis as justifying exclusivity for his own point of view—"let it be tested by the Bible," he said.

No biblical theology, or theologian, tries to establish an either-my-way-or-else on his own authority. But LT does!

Listen:

"None of these various kinds of men," Enzo Gatti says of those who do not share his LT perspectives, "are [*sic*] capable of being followers of Yahweh, the God of human freedom" (37:8). So much for such triflers!

Instead of submitting to his Church, and opening himself to learning from its teaching magisterium, Gatti undertakes to reverse roles and mounts as it were a kind of papacy of his own: "The Church will be saved only if it seeks out and pursues the poor, choosing and coopting them as the privileged citizens of the kingdom. They are the Church's only salvation" (37:121). "*Only,*" no less! Man, not God, is the "Church's only salvation!" LT deals in absolutes—its own!

God Himself can be heard *exclusively* where the Liberation Theologian hears Him. So says José Miranda: "The God who does not allow himself to be objectified, because only in the immediate command of conscience is he God, clearly specifies that he is knowable exclusively in the cry of the poor and the weak who seek justice" (66:48). Note that "exclusively!" Miranda says further, "'Knowledge of Jahweh' cannot be understood if we do not realize that it is a strict synonym for the realization of justice" (66:51). "Cannot be understood," that is, unless heard in the accents of Marx!

Presuming to exegete the Epistles of John, Miranda says, "John's intention is clearly directed to maintaining that God is knowable only through one's neighbor" (66:64). "Only" through one's neighbor? Really? Does not this same John report Christ's saying, "No one comes to the Father [not by way of the neighbor] but by me" (John 14:6)?

The Bible clearly teaches that God chooses to be known in a variety of ways: in the Christ, in His Word, through His creation, and then served in the neighbor!

"The only thing he understands as sin," says Miranda, writing of St. Paul's Romans, "with respect to content, is injustice. . . ." (66:170). Still, the "only. . . ." Miranda here confuses sin with evil, and misrepresents St. Paul besides.

What Paul does teach is that all human evil, including injustice, rises out of the sin of deliberate refusal to acknowledge God as creator and Lord. And this sin leads not only to injustice, but to a wide variety of evils, listed by Paul for Miranda to ponder in Romans, chapter 1, verses 29-32.

The ideologist casually sets his own infallibility above that of the Bible to suit his convenience. Hear Fierro's version of this unique display of insolence: ". . . whether those who reported the event in the

Bible were aware of it or not . . . the Exodus from Egypt was a political act, clearly bearing the stamp of resistance and rebellion" (33:147).

"In Moltmann's theology," Fierro writes of the German exponent of political theology, "we find an intransigent eschatological exclusivism that allows us to meet God only in the promise, the future, and hope" (33:263).

"Allows us to meet God . . ," no less, but only where the Liberationist wills Him to be found! How profound a grace that the Church is not bound by the Liberation Theologian's "intransigeance!"—how profound an impudence that the Liberationist thinks even God Himself is!

Juan Luis Segundo, Catholic Liberationist of Uruguay, has it that LT could not even theologize using "the same concept of God, sin, sacrament, and church membership that was part of a church centered around the quest for extraterrestrial salvation" (33:354).

But in truth the Church is not centered on "extraterrestrial salvation." He is confusing the Body of Christ, perhaps for rhetorical purposes, with parachurch folk who make a good terrestrial living by peddling debentures on extraterrestrial mansions! But who, except the ideologist blinded by his own limitations, confuses parachurch with the Church?

Emilio Castro, recently appointed Secretary General of the World Council of Churches, pushes exclusivism to its ultimate by saying that *only* those who stand with LT, on LT's exclusive terms, have any claim to doing theology: "Either the theologian is a human being committed to the struggle for liberation or he is not a theologian" (33:386). Sign up, or sign out!

Alfredo Fierro frankly equates LT exclusivism with its Marxist assumptions: "Not every option is reasonable . . . One must choose the partisanship that is destined for universality. In Marxist theory it is the working class that provides that partisanship. As Marx saw it, the proletariat is the class that contains the seed for the dissolution of all classes, that cannot emancipate itself without emancipating society as a whole. In a word, the proletariat is the universal class. Acceptance of this Marxist hypothesis explains why the theologians of liberation and revolution tell Christians they must make a class option, and why they envision something so seemingly one-sided and partisan as a 'leftist theology' " 33:386-87). LT intends to play on the winning side!

LT blazons, however, its claims to exclusive novelty: "All this," says Gutierrez, "means entering a very different world. It gives rise to a new and unheard-of type of Christian experience . . ." (43:14).

Note on "Identification" and Integrity

Liberation Theologians, the reader soon observes, are fond of announcing—if not boasting of—their "identification" with the poor. Only those who do so, they insist, can really pursue theological reflection.

It is *only,* LT repeats over and over, out of the "matrix" of shared poverty and oppression that genuine "theological reflection" can flower. This is a convenient technique for ruling out in advance any reflections that run counter to LT's own.

Hear, for example, Gustavo Gutierrez: "We turn this history into one of authentic communion when we opt for the poor and exploited classes, identify ourselves with their plight, and share their fate. There is no other way to accept the gratuitous gift of sonship" (39:16). The usual: "No other way!" Which happens to be the Marxist way!

But just what do the Liberationists mean by their "identification" with the poor and oppressed? What, precisely, does Gutierrez mean by sharing the "fate" of the poor? Does he mean, as one would innocently suppose, taking up residence in their hovels, eating their crusts, risking their ailments?

His meaning becomes not a little evasive as one pursues his explanation of it to the very end of his "classic" treatise.

It begins to appear that "sharing the fate" of the poor may not denote living as, and with, the impoverished, at one with them in material and spiritual destitution.

No, "sharing their fate" may not require that because "Material poverty," Gutierrez says, "is a scandalous condition."

Granted it is so, but does the Liberationist mean, then, Why should he court scandal? This is not the way he intends to "share the fate" of the poor? Apparently not, as we shall see.

Will he share, then, if not the material poverty then the spiritual indigence of the exploited?

Again, it does not seem so.

Gutierrez goes on to say that "spiritual poverty" is a "spiritual childhood" (43:299)—presumably unfit for the adult theologian too?

Therefore, he says, "We have laid aside these first two meanings."

The Liberationist well nigh boasts of "sharing the fate" of the poor, but rules out meaning material or spiritual poverty? Can that be?

Gutierrez is almost open about it: assuming material poverty, he says, "would be to aspire to a condition which is recognized as degrading to man. It would be, moreover, to move against the current of history . . . [and] would be to justify, even involuntarily, the injustice and exploitation which is the cause of poverty" (43:299).

Does this mean what it seems to say? The Liberation Theologian cannot really accept material poverty because: 1) that would be "degrading" to himself; 2) that would be moving "against" the current of history; and 3) that would mean he "justifies" the system he denounces?

But what remains, now, of this indispensable "identification" with the poor, and "sharing their fate," lacking which, theologians are—on LT grounds—incapacitated for theological reflection?

Gutierrez may think he answers the question by saying, "Spiritual poverty means above all total availability to the Lord" (43:299). Ah, *this* is a form of sharing "the fate" of the poor which the Liberation Theologian has no difficulty in ascribing to himself.

So, what remains when the verbal haze has settled seems to be only this: the Liberation Theologian expresses his identification with the oppressed, 1) through a "total availability" to the Lord, which apparently exempts him from living with the impoverished; and 2) through a "commitment to witness!" This, Gutierrez declares, is his "expression of love, is solidarity *with the poor* and is a protest *against poverty*" (italics his, 43:300-301).

We come full circle: identification with the "fate" of the poor turns out in "praxis" simply to be a "witness in protest against poverty!" Leave it to the dialectician to have it both ways! But let Gutierrez put it his way:

"And so there are emerging new ways of living poverty which are different from the classic 'renunciation of the goods of this world' " (43:301).

"New ways"—not to say cheap ways!—of stripping "identification" of what it denotes, while wielding it as a weapon against all other "reflections."

But if "witness" for God and against human evil, for divine (not Marxist) justice on behalf of those whom Franz Fannon called "the wretched of the earth" is what the Liberation Theologian means by sharing the "fate" of the poor, there is nothing "new" about it! Across the centuries, without boasting it a virtue indispensable to theologizing, the Church has "witnessed" against exploitation in language so powerful as to pale even the strongest rhetoric of Marx, let alone the turgid stuff LT produces.

There is a Word which does "witness" for the poor, one which, it must be confessed, Latin American pulpits have not trumpeted as loudly and universally as both rich and poor require. It is the Word of the Lord, preached from faithful pulpits and demanding of all men and women an obedience from which alone social justice can be anticipated.

That Word addresses man as man, whatever his possessions, wherever his "class." And the Last Judgment guaranteed by that Word (Matt. 25:31-46) knows only two identifications: those on the Lord's right hand and those on His left—an "identification" achieved through obedience or rebellion!

We will talk about that Word in the last section of this study.

Hear one more voice: "Only among those who are actually working and fighting to overcome social conflict for the benefit of all will we get langauge and symbols that can serve as the vehicle for the universality of the church's message of faith in Christ" (39:89). The "word" according to Luis G. del Valle. And again, "Only . . ." among Liberationists!

With a particularly ironic illustration of LT exclusivism we will close the door on this unsavory facet of "theological reflection."

José Comblin insists, as do other Liberation Theologians in offhand ways, that "God's wisdom has been revealed to the poor, the ignorant, the weak, and the rejected." This is, he adds, "not an abstract fact to be contemplated, but a program to be applied" (18:6).

Suppose, now, that we take him seriously and at his word.

True "wisdom" is found only among the poor. So LT says.

If LT *means* just that, then will not LT publications fairly bristle with words of divine wisdom drawn from the lips of the poor, if not conveyed in the actual accents of the poor?

Doesn't LT boast of its finding the "matrix" of "theological reflection" where it identifies with the poor? And if here wisdom is to be found, LT will surely purvey it in quantity to its followers.

But one searches in vain for even one syllable which Comblin has transcribed, and just one insight LT confesses to have learned, from those "poor and oppressed" to whom "God's wisdom has been revealed," and with whom LT so blatantly, and exclusively, affirms identification.

What the reader does find is that Comblin and Company are bent upon telling the poor—and the world—their own ideas, not upon listening for a word from the Lord in the depths of poverty. The poor are, for LT as they are for Marxism, but tokens in the deadly serious game of political propaganda. The "poor" furnish the propaganda weapon used to beat the Establishment about the head—and conscience! That LT really finds them a repository of divine wisdom is, judging by LT praxis, but a pose. Where does the reader find, in LT publications, starting with the writing of Comblin himself, something to the effect, "This I learned from the poor," or "This I was taught by the oppressed"? He finds nothing!

This raises a question of intellectual honesty, which cannot be lightly dismissed. Is LT's exclusivistic preoccupation with "the poor" genuine or an ideological device?

Gutierrez does, after 300 pages of his own "reflection," make some acknowledgement that a problem exists:

"In the last instance we will have an authentic theology of liberation only when the oppressed themselves can freely raise their voice and express themselves directly and creatively in society and in the heart of the People of God."

But if this means what it says, then Gutierrez is confessing that as of now we do *not* have "an authentic theology of liberation . . . !" LT is, to date, less than such an "authentic theology!"

A moment of truth as refreshing as it is rare. But read on:

"For now we must limit ourselves to efforts which ought to deepen and support that process, which has barely begun" (43:307). What "process"? If it is the "process" of arriving at the point where the "oppressed" can articulate "an authentic theology of liberation," then what is it that masquerades under that name now?

Or, is this, too, a pose? Are the "oppressed" so inarticulate today as to have nothing to say via the lips of Liberation Theologians, IF those Theologians were really interested in what the poor have to say? Has any Liberationist actually advised his colleagues to harken to the voice of the ghetto in lieu of producing yet another treatise of his own?

Or is all this not, in fact, but another version of the Marxist-fostered delusion that some day the proletariat will be permitted to rise to self-determination and self-expression? If, that is, they follow the Marxist oriented "process" promoted by LT today!

As for Marxism, so for LT, the "poor" serve only to give a semblance of popular concern to what is in fact a totalitarian, undemocratic, tyrannical ideology, so exclusively obsessed with its own objectives as to rule out any other perspective.

2. Immoderately Ours!

Like all ideologists, the Liberation Theologian is not only exclusivist. He essentially postulates his own omniscience, sufficiently so that the reader will soon hear one Liberationist propose to call "other Christians" to judgment before the bar of LT!

José Miranda is so assured of his own originality that he dares to say, "Paul's gospel has nothing to do with the interpretation which has for centuries been given to it in terms of individual salvation. It deals with the justice which the world and peoples and society, implicitly but anxiously, have been waiting" (66:179). A writer who flippantly dismisses "centuries" of Pauline exegesis in favor of his own interpretation makes the head swim. Ideology does that to people, even theologians.

Miranda sets himself equally above most Marxists: "Since this ignorance of the meaning of 'dialectics' also plagues the overwhelming majority of Marxists, they themselves have facilitated such a great falsification of Marx's thought" (66:259)!

How did the Church, and the Marxists, stumble along before LT brightened the horizon?

Hugo Assmann sits in judgment thus: "In view of the appalling political naivete of much theology, it can at least be suggested that using secular science as a basis for theological reflection may be the only realistic way of dragging theology out of its ghetto" (5:64). What kind of abysmal ignorance of the history of the Church can underlie such braggadocio? Were the Fathers who withstood emperors, the Popes who subdued kings, the Puritans who led revolutions unaware of the political implications of theology?! And how cheap a gesture: all but Liberation Theologians consigned to some "ghetto"—wherever that may be.

Small wonder that in his encounter with LT at Puebla, Pope John Paul II was constrained to remind his priests and Bishops of what some seemed determined to forget: "Those familiar with the history of the Church [did the Pope mean to imply that some of those clerics before him were deliberately ignorant of their own Church's past?] know that in every age there have been admirable bishops deeply involved in the valiant defense of the human dignity of those entrusted to them by the Lord. Their activity was always mandated by their episcopal mission, because they regarded human dignity as a gospel value that cannot be despised without greatly offending the Creator" (30:65).

One of those of whom the Pope was well aware, José Comblin, has no problem with referring to Liberation Theologians as the "most enlightened and conscious sectors of the church . . ." (18:98), and undertakes single-handed to develop further the work of a whole Council: "The following considerations are a continuation, or extension, of Vatican II ecclesiology, not a simple application" (18:181).

To this formidable theological enterprise Comblin thinks he brings a special qualification: "What does the New Testament really say when it is read liberated from the ideologies of the past and the temptations of the present" (18:185)?

And who presents himself as qualified to make such a purified reading?

José Comblin, of course!

There is an immoderate aspect to Liberation Theology, promoted, though the Theologian is unaware of that, by its ideological stance.

PART **IV**

Why *Not* Liberation Theology?

As pastors, you keenly realize that your chief duty is to be teachers of truth: not of a human, rational truth but of the truth that comes from God. That truth includes the principle of authentic human liberation: "You will know the truth, and the truth will set you free" (John 8:32). It is the one and only truth that offers a solid basis for an adequate praxis.

The truth we owe to human beings is, first and foremost, a truth about themselves. . . . We cannot reduce it to the principles of some philosophical system, or to a mere political activity.

Whatever the miseries or sufferings that afflict human beings, it is not through violence, power-plays, or political systems but through the truth about human beings that they will find their way to a better future.

Pope John Paul II, at Puebla, Mexico

There is nothing in the Latin American system, to which the liberation theologians point, for which Marxism affords the only or the best explanation. It offers no "method" either of inquiry or of action by which modern life is to be better understood, its future predicted, or its utopian hopes realized.

Michael Novak

10

Liberation Theology Ab-Uses the Bible

We have observed so far that LT structures itself upon the four pillars of Marxism, all the while insisting upon its exclusive and well-nigh infallible originality.

We have noted, also, that LT looks for the sources of its "theological reflection" almost anywhere but in the Scriptures and the creeds, dismissing these as outmoded.

For many this is ground enough for rejecting Liberation Theology.

But some readers will want to know what "practical" difference an effort to blend Marxism and Christianity makes. This especially in the light of vigorous efforts by World Council of Churches representatives and others to promote Marxist-Christian "dialogue" for a better "understanding" of Marxism, to the benefit, supposedly, of the Church.

A typical attempt to make Marxist-Christian conversations apparently profitable, and incidentally to make Marxism more palatable to the American reader, is the volume titled *Christians & The Many Faces Of Marxism,* edited by Wayne Stumme out of a series of papers presented to a "major consultation" sponsored by the Lutheran World Federation in 1983.

The thrust of the compilation can be caught from its Foreword: "If Western institutions, including Christian churches, continue to participate in the exploitation of people and raw materials in Asia, Africa, and Latin America, the people of these countries will have no alternative but to turn for help to those who espouse some form of Marxist ideology" (82:13).

The reader will recognize in this sweeping indictment a form of intellectual blackmail of the "When did you stop beating your wife?" variety. By this standard, LT has already far-sightedly turned for "help" to Marxism. And since the essays in this collection assume that in fact the West only exploits the rest of the world, and suggest no practical ways in which the Church could extricate itself from implication in the process, the concluding writer will naturally be saying: "Such oppression—the denial of all that we understand freedom to be—cannot be permitted to continue. . . . Christians should seek to make common cause with those who work to end such oppression" (82:146)—"common cause," that is with Marxism!

Oddly enough—or isn't it?—the writer is not thinking of the denial of freedom behind the Iron Curtain! She has in view the "oppressed" of the Western world!

Because, however, ideology demands absolute sovereignty in whatever partnerships it shares, what does turning to Marxism for "help" cost?

We will in this chapter and the next review what LT "pays" for its alliance with Marxism as tool and as partner.

The first payment—we will call them "sacrifices"—to Marx is, as already noticed, the authority of the Bible.

Ideology recognizes no center of authority beside itself. LT has to choose: the word of Marx or the Word of God.

It chooses: the word of Marx!

How, then, does LT view the Bible?

We have seen that LT wrests from the Bible only what fits its Marxist structure. This is LT in "praxis." But what does the Liberation Theologian say about the Bible, which Christians have universally accepted as inspired and infallible source of the doctrines they believe true?

Listen to Hugo Assmann: "How can we talk candidly of the 'gospel' when there is so much truth in what one committed Christian once said to me: 'The Bible? It doesn't exist. The only Bible is the sociological bible of what I see happening here and now as a Christian'?" (5:61).

Plain enough: "The Bible? It doesn't exist."

One might be curious to know how either the speaker being quoted or the "theologian" quoting him knows what being a "Christian" is if there be no Bible to define Christianity for us. But it is at least clear that for Assmann there is no Bible to discipline his "theological reflection"—nor, then, to give it a foundation other than his own assertion! The Bible "doesn't exist."

Assmann quotes his anonymous "Christian" to lend authority to a conclusion he has already enunciated on his own, as follows:

"It is impossible to go straight to the 'heart of Christianity' because Christianity exists only in a series of historical embodiments; if the Bible itself is not a direct source of criteria, but the history of successive interpretations, always partial and sometimes directly contradictory, of these criteria; if the conjuncture of word and deed is essential to the concept of revelation; and if, furthermore, all this has come down to us formed, deformed, reformed and deformed again by the actual history of Christianity; and if the differing historical circumstances in which Christianity has found itself have produced their own formulations of dogma, canon law and pastoral practice; then how can we talk simply of criteria perceived 'in the light of faith' "? (5:60-61).

The maze of qualifications is hardly intended to clarify what the Liberationist thinks he is freeing himself from, but the end result is obvious: the Bible is useless as a "matrix" for "theological reflection"— "formed, deformed, reformed and deformed again"—poor thing!

And where, then, does LT's "theological reflection" turn for its source of truth? With the arrogance characteristic of ideology, Assmann finds the answer to that question astonishingly close to home:

"The original 'text' has become our reality and our practice" (5:104).

Perhaps one has to read that twice, or more, to escape astonishment, if not outrage. But it is simply what we have already been saying, namely, that the theologian who negates the Bible has no source for his affirmations beyond himself. Assmann illustrates precisely what Marxism "costs" Liberation Theology: the "text" *is* actually the theologian's own "reality" and "practice" stabilized after a fashion by quotation from Marx.

Who would admit the need of a Bible if *his* reality and *his* practice are become the voice of Truth? Who, with such an estimate of himself, would heed the "deformed" Scriptures if he acknowledged its existence?

Would it be by coincidence that no one else can read or dispute the interpretation of a "text" if it be lodged deep in the theologian's own consciousness? Rather neat, in a way: "my" text says. . . .

"Did God say?" the Devil once wanted to know, well aware of what God had said (Gen. 3:1). The device remains ever the same, and the Liberation Theologian, like the Serpent, already knows the answer he wants. Not what God said, but what "I" say. If it were so (as certainly in authentic theologizing it is not!) that, to repeat, "the 'text' is our situation, and our situation is our primary and basic reference point," then all the others—the Bible, the creeds, the magisterium or teaching authority of the Church and the history of dogma take second place, or less. LT roves the skies of speculation on its own, and mistakes such license for freedom!

Not always quite so cavalier, but no more responsive to the authority of the inspired Word, other Liberation Theologians employ the device of "rereading" the Bible. This does not imply more careful study of the text to discover better its meaning. Rather "rereading" means in practice that LT puts its own construction upon texts which in themselves have never been understood in ways that bless LT ideology.

By "reread" understand, then, "extract the meaning we want." Or, more accurately, by "reread" understand the meaning which a commitment to Marxist "help" requires.

For example, LT has been, Gutierrez declares, "By renewed involvement in politics led to a rereading of the gospel message" (39:13). What he means, of course, is not that LT discovers words that were not there before. No, the text simply acquires from LT a new and favorable orientation to Marxism. Gutierrez says frankly enough: "What is involved here is precisely that: a rereading of the gospel message from within the context of liberaton praxis" (39:25). That is plain enough: from within the context established by commitment to Marxist rebellion, the gospel is "re-read" to say what Marxism permits the Liberation Theologian to hear!

Raul Vidales puts it this way: "This same perspective obliges the theologian to re-read the Bible from the context of the other 'Bible' known as human history. It is one dialectical activity, not two separate, parallel tasks" (39:40). Another re-reader! LT hears the Bible only in dialectical accents! In practice, "one dialectical activity," means that the "other" Bible, seen through Marxist lenses, lays down the norms and gives the marching orders governing both 'Bibles'—as ideology always does! In being "reread" the Bible loses both its priority and its authority!

Having, however, smothered the Bible in dialectical embrace, Vidales still wants his readers to believe that he acknowledges its supreme authority as God's Word, saying: "But how can theology manage to maintain its critical function so that it will subvert and relativize would-be absolutes? It can only do so insofar as it continues to refer back to its vital underlying source and principle: the word of God. . . . It is a critical-minded theory operating in the light of God's word as accepted by faith and motivated by a practical intention. . . . This biblical perspective places liberation theology within the most solid and sound tradition of Christian theology. The preeminent function of Scripture is indisputable, as is the functional character of the church and the magisterium and their service role" (39:47-48).

As on other occasions, one wonders here if the Liberationist is serious. How little LT "theological reflection" accords with "the most solid and sound tradition of Christian theology," will be shown in our next chapter. The reader can then decide how much weight to accord to Vidales' assertion of fidelity to the inspired Word.

Luis G. del Valle also rereads Scripture: "After hearing the word of God in the concrete events of today, we would compare it with the word of God that was heard in the events of a past day. In particular, we would compare it with the word of God that echoed in the supreme event: Jesus Christ, the Word made flesh" (39:85).

Attend thoughtfully, reader, to what this Liberationist says: *first,* LT assumes its competence to hear "the word of God in the concrete events of today"—as perceived, no doubt, in the Marxist categories it has expressly adopted for purposes of analysis. LT thus undertakes to write its own 'Bible.' Then LT makes a comparison of such personalized hearing of God's "word" with the inspired revelation recorded in the true Bible, a comparison degrading to the original version.

"The most solid and sound tradition of Christian theology"—to quote Vidales—drawing its authority from the Bible, teaches that the biblical writers who heard the Word of God and committed it to writing enjoyed the guiding hand of the Holy Spirit. So the Bible says (II Tim. 3:16; II Pet. 1:21). The Liberationist sets his listening on a par—or indeed above—that inspired by the Holy Spirit! It follows that LT will come to claiming its own hearing Spirit-guided—as we shall see!

Leonardo Boff casually equates the Liberation Theologian with Christ Himself as both equally "listeners" to the "word" as revealed in daily events.

Boff writes: "In the eyes of the prophet from Nazareth, the will of God is not to be found solely in the classic texts of Scripture. Life itself is the place where God's salvific will for human beings is made manifest" (39:118).

Both the Liberationist and the Christ are equals, reading out the "word" of God from off the events of the day! Boff is twice mistaken: 1) he flies in the face of the Lord's repeated explanation that He walks according to the "it is written" in the "Scriptures," not what He finds in "life itself;" and, 2) if God did intend us to find His "salvific will" in "life itself," He would not have troubled to inspire and preserve the Bible. Boff's arrogance, however, obviously denigrates the authority of the Bible by elevating LT's "words" to its same source.

Each Liberationist becomes, finally, his own bible. He "hears" it, "writes" it, interprets it and pledges himself for its novelty.

Why, we will wonder once again, in the light of LT's "dialectical hermeneutics," does the Liberation Theologian want—except to fool the credulous—to extract some grudging concessions from the Bible, some faint nod of approval from that (to him) ancient, outdated, unreliable word? Some perusal, for example, of the tortuous expositions to be found in Miranda's *Marx And The Bible* leaves one pondering the inexplicable oddity as of a modern Esau's pursuing a blessing from an aged Jacob grown old and blind to the ways of modern man. What normative difference would it make, in Miranda's or LT's ideological theorizing, if Marx and the Bible were wholly at odds or wholly at one? Marx in the end is always enough!

We may understand, now, why LT universally insists that theology is the theologians' critical reflection upon his own situation. He makes of himself the source of his own authority, and of his situation his only point of reference. His is the hearing, the rereading, the reflecting. And his is the "word" which gains, he seems to think, in authentication by his denigrating that of Holy Scripture.

Note on Word and Spirit

All who "liberate" their "theological reflection" from the Bible develop a two-pronged justification for their heresy: 1) they disparage the "letter," and 2) claim the personal illumination of the Holy Spirit. This is a sectarian phenomenon as old as the Church.

There is no doubt that LT disparages the letter—"deformed. . . . etc." LT pays no attention to whatever the Bible says which is out of step with its ideology.

And, like all sectarians, LT transcends (it thinks) the Bible by laying claim to immediate revelations of the Spirit. In praxis, this comes to mean that whenever the Bible declines to say what they want to hear, the sects have taken the easy route to get where they want to go: the Holy Spirit drops by to teach them!

An illustration of this transposition can be found in a recent work of German theologian Jürgen Moltmann, whose *Theology Of Hope* stimulated the development of Liberation Theology. In more recent work, *The Church In The Power Of The Spirit* (67), Moltmann seems only to be saying what "Moltmann in the power of the Spirit" has to teach the Church!

So too with Liberation Theology.

Like many deviations which have tried to traduce the Church, LT flies the banner of the Spirit. Who, vouchsafed such "revelation," would dare disobey the inner witness of God's Spirit! Who so foolish as to hobble along with the ancient letter while the living Spirit lends wings to every eccentricity!

We really need not linger long to observe this self-serving (or, better, Marxism-serving) fiction at work in LT.

Fiction?

Yes, fiction! The "solid tradition" Christian theology teaches across the centuries what the Bible teaches concerning the role of the Spirit as regards revealing Truth: 1) the Spirit inspires the biblical authors to commit the Word of the Lord to the repository of language; 2) the

Spirit illumines the meaning of that language upon the minds of all who come to the Word, eager to obey. So the Church has long held in struggles with the "enthusiasts," the name commonly given to deviants claiming Spirit-given revelations.

"When the Spirit of truth comes," Jesus says, "he will guide you into all truth . . . ;" and by stopping here the advocates of new, Spirit-given revelations claim support for their wildest theorizings. But the Lord does not stop there! He goes on to say: "For he will not speak on his own authority, but whatever he hears he will speak . . . He will glorify me, for he will take what is mine and declare it to you" (John 16:13-14). The Spirit invents no "new" revelations. The Word the Spirit brought to the writers of the Bible is the Word of the Lord! Jesus makes that very clear:

The work of the Spirit will be to "bring to your remembrance all that I have said to you" (John 14:26). What the Spirit did bring to the Apostles' remembrance joined the Old Testament as God's inspired and infallible Word. And when the Bible thus constituted comes to its conclusion, the final inspired scribe, St. John, expressly warns against claiming the authority to add anything to the Word:

"I warn every one who hears the words of the prophecy of this book: if any one adds to them, God will add to him the plagues described in this book, and if any one takes away from the words of the book of this prophecy, God will take away his share in the tree of life and in the holy city, which are described in this book" (Rev. 22:18-19). The Church has applied these frightening anathemas to the whole of Scripture, declaring in theological language, that thus the canon of Scripture was closed, and whatever insights anyone claims thereafter can be accredited only as they agree with the Bible.

But the ideological mind, emboldened by various "rereadings" of St. John's warning, has across the centuries of ecclesiastical sectarianism (see Msgr. Ronald Knox's *Enthusiasm* [48], for example), claimed unique Spirit-given revelations. So, now, does LT. Hear José Comblin:

The "concept of Christian liberation," he says, "is not specified in the New Testament. But that does not matter" (19:159).

Note two things: 1) the New Testament does not authorize LT's "concept of Christian liberation!"—a confession as remarkable as it is of no consequence, for it is immediately brushed aside; 2) that this "does not matter," is as telling a revelation of LT's attitude toward the Bible as it a nonchalant display of arrogance that would shock us, were it not already an LT trademark.

Comblin continues, "The truths of Christianity are composed of the revelation both of Jesus Christ and of the Spirit. Both divine persons are necessary; they are the two hands of the Father accomplishing his plan" (18:159). It must not be mistakenly supposed that here Comblin is repeating what we have heard the Lord saying through St. John, that the Spirit will "take from" Him and reveal that to us. On the contrary, in LT praxis this comes to mean that what LT cannot discover in the "hand" of Jesus as revealed in the Bible, LT will attribute to the "hand" of the Spirit as guiding the ideologist. An absolutely no-lose posture for the wildest flights of "theological reflection!" That the Spirit seems to speak with the accents of Karl Marx is, for LT, no surprise.

Hear Comblin further, reflecting LT's obsession with the term *new:* "The new theology has a new understanding of itself and, therefore, a new subject. Its aim is no longer to discover a system of ideas, but to enlighten and judge the action of Christians."

And by what authority does LT dare to "judge the action of Christians"? And to set itself at whim against the Bible, the creeds, the Vatican, the magisterium, and the Church's traditions?

You can guess, reader. LT claims its own revelation!

We read on in Comblin:

"This new theology . . . seeks to connect God's word to the present circumstance in order to express what God's word is saying to human beings who are engaged in concrete processes. The rationale for this change is the new understanding that Christ did not come to teach a system of ideas but only to help humankind to be saved. Christ's word means concrete actions in the present time" (18:48-49).

What LT means by "concrete actions" we now well know. They are those dictated by the Marxist ideology which LT has adopted as its own.

And now the secret comes out, as Comblin joins LT with the sectarians: "Freedom is a new life, a new behavior. Its principle lies within the human person; it proceeds from his or her will, from the Spirit living within each person's heart. The new behavior is not unreasonable, indeed, it is reason itself; the 'new man' is guided by the Spirit . . ." (18:147).

The Marxist-LT "new man" (somewhat to Marx's surprise, considering Feuerbach!) enjoys nothing less than the guidance of the Holy Spirit!

The Church has endured much over many centuries from sectarians claiming that their wildest delusions were Spirit-inspired. LT only joins a long-discredited line of fringe enthusiasts.

The "spirit," however, who inspires the LT vision of a "new man" is that of Marx, not the Third Person of the Holy Trinity.

It must be added that efforts at the wayward manipulation of the Holy Spirit is courting a "sin" which the Lord strenuously warns us to avoid: "Therefore I tell you, every sin and blasphemy will be forgiven men, but the blasphemy against the Spirit will not be forgiven . . . either in this age or in the age to come" (Matt. 12:31-32). To claim that any man's reading of "life" reveals the "salvific will of God" and enjoys the authority of the Holy Spirit—is this not risking blasphemy?!

But what is one to think of an assertion like this unseemly expression of Enzo Gatti's: "To believe means to possess the Spirit of Christ. To believe means to draw upon all one's inner energies, as stirred up and set in movement precisely by the Spirit, in order to give the Christ-event a new incarnation at every moment and to speak that event forth to others" (37:58). If words are taken at face value, this Liberation Theologian not only attributes his speech to the Spirit, but presents himself as a reincarnation of the Christ!

The Greeks had a term for this kind of insensate pride. Those who foolishly imagined themselves equal to the gods were, by way of divine revenge, infected with what the Greek called *hubris,* the gigantic pride that assays scaling Olympus, home of the gods—and precedes ignominious fall. Which led to the aphorism, "Those whom the gods would destroy they first make mad." But how mild is the madness of equating oneself with the deities of Olympus in comparison with the delusion of ab-using the Spirit for drawing upon "one's inner energies" to duplicate the "Christ-event!"

Liberation Theology presumes to energize Marxism with the power of a God Marx was at pains to deny. And Marx's denial inheres in his recognition that the God of the Scriptures abides no such subjugation to ideology. How well Marx knew, deep in a heritage stemming from Moses and Prophets, that the God of Israel was a "jealous God" (Deut. 5:8), sharing sovereignty with none! Marx was at pains, therefore, to insist that the God of the Bible does not exist! Marx's atheism was as forthright as LT's playing games with Bible and Spirit and the Christ is devious.

Among those absent from Marxist-Christian exercises in dialogue where the well-fed discuss the hungry and the well-clothed empathize with the naked would be Karl Marx! Just as among those repudiating an LT amalgam of ideology and Christianity would be . . . Karl Marx!

What critique beyond its own extravagance is necessary to evaluate an ideology that claims such intimacy with the Spirit as sufficient to set its words on par with the Bible, that claims duplication in the theologian of Christ's incarnation, that claims authority to judge Christians, that dismisses as "no matter" the absence of its presumably "theological" motifs in the New Testament?

11

Basic Doctrines Perverted by Concession to Marxism

Liberation Theology takes its structure from Marxism.

In payment for this ideological "help," LT either dismisses the Bible altogether or lets the ideology warp the inspired text through "re-reading" it.

In consequence, LT's alliance with Marxism costs the sacrifice of all the basic constituents of "the most solid and sound tradition of Christian theology!"

We will consider ten of these doctrinal casualties:

1. First Victim: The Doctrine of the Fall

Marxism has no doctrine of the Fall. Neither, therefore, has LT!

The Bible teaches that God made His creation good, man included.

Placed in Eden's garden, mandated to till and care for it, man received from his Creator a "probationary" command: "You may eat freely of every tree of the garden, but of the tree of the knowledge of good and evil you shall not eat, for in the day that you eat of it you shall die" (Gen. 2:16).

Would man, made free and in the Image of God, validate his freedom through obedience, or prefer the illusion of license and "liberate" himself and all mankind into slavery to the Devil?

Adam and Eve defied God's Word!

Rebellion was born in Eden and has infected ideology ever since.

God indicted man's sin and cast him out of the garden. This is the biblical account, revealed in the early chapters of Genesis and taken for granted in the Bible thereafter.

As a consequence of man's sin, a "depravity" consisting in the propensity to reject God and to inflict evil upon one's neighbor entered the life blood of all mankind. This, according to the Scriptures, is the source of all the evil that Marx—and LT—attributes to class struggle.

It is in the context of man's original sin, with all the incalculable human misery in its train, that the story of Israel, and the divine promise of redemption through the incarnation, suffering, death and resurrection of Jesus Christ find their significance—to become the inspired gospel of redemption. God redeems man, as illustrated in God's liberation of Israel from Egypt. Without the doctrine of the Fall, the story of the Exodus becomes—as indeed it is in the hands of Liberation Theologians—but an inexplicable whim of an unpredictable deity. Why Egypt? Why Israel? And, above all, why a purely temporal liberation destined to drain away into the sands of the desert?

Or does it all take on profound symbolic significance because, as the Bible teaches, God's own Son was already in the loins of Israel, validating for both Israel and Jesus, with all that means for man's true liberation: "Out of Egypt have I called my son" (Hos. 11:1, Matt. 2:15)!

But Marxism sets the pace which LT meekly adopts by rejecting not only the Bible but also any notion of the Fall, probably for at least two reasons:

1) The doctrine of the Fall and its lamentable consequence is all-encompassing. No one is left unscathed. All mankind suffers the inherited taint. But this includes Marx and the Marxists! The "Prophet" (which means seer!) himself—if the Fall be admitted—suffers inherited myopic vision; the Marxist physician must first attend to himself. This is a test which ideology and ideologists cannot abide. Theirs must be, as we have already heard, the voice of unquestioned and unquestionable authority, addressed to mankind from a sanctuary immune to the intrusion of doubt or error. For Marxist ideology, then, the doctrine of the Fall, like the Bible itself, must be myth.

2) Moreover the Fall deprives man of all capacity for self-redemption. How could the innately deficient re-new himself? Human history, according to the Bible, lost in Eden the resources for man's self-redemption. Only from outside the scope of time can true healing come. All this Marx must repudiate, or surrender his ideology.

And we have already observed what his alternative is: he locates the source of human evil within the boundaries of history, and believes that as historical circumstances are deliberately altered, human evil will be done away—by new men creating a new era along Marxist lines.

LT accepts the Marxist lead, and obligingly removes from its expurgated Bible all reference to man's Fall!

The reader searches LT treatises in vain for any recognition of the debacle in Eden. None of those who figure so prominently in the early pages (and elsewhere) of the Scriptures receives LT recognition: no First Adam (whom St. Paul relates so significantly to Jesus, the Second Adam), no Eve, no tree, no Eden, no temptor, no probationary command, no Fall, and therefore no primal promise (Gen. 3:15) of vicarious redemption—all blotted out of LT's version of the Bible!

Why?

It's the price LT is willing to pay for the Marxist program of human self-redemption through rebellion! And more, so LT can pose, like Marxism, with an authority untainted by inheritance from a fallen progenitor. The LT Bible bends as the Marxist wind blows.

And so LT exposes itself to the same fate already befallen Marxism wherever it takes historical form as Communism. Though born of great genius and immense self-denial, though inspired by a vision of a new humanity born with a boundlessly progressive future, Marxism in practice always gives rise to the dull, gray brutalism of the totalitarian state. Why?

Well, when the "old" man, inheritor of the depravity visited upon humankind by Adam's transgression, seizes dictatorial power for the purpose of making others "new," (deluding himself that he is "new" already!), the fact of his unredeemed depravity is soon writ large in the horrors of Gulag, murder and unrelieved oppression. Whatever may have been the chains and slavery of pre-Marxist societies—in Russia, in China, in Cuba, in Vietnam, everywhere—the shackles forged by Communism are more binding, more absolute, more pervasive and more deadly than the revolution swept away. The more loudly Marxism denies human depravity in words, the more resolutely Marxism-in-action demonstrates its own depravity in deeds. It will not be otherwise wherever LT engineers the rebellions it schemes for.

Self-blinded, however, to this patent testimony of history, LT joins Marxists in rejecting the Fall:

Hear José Comblin: "God's image is the freedom of men and women, the simple little seed of freedom that has never disappeared" (18:110). "Never disappeared"! The phrase is Arminian, but implies here that there was no Fall! Yes, the divine image, given freely to man, endowed him with freedom. But what LT ignores is that man as he was made is no longer man as he is. There *was* a Fall!

Jesuit Pierre Bigo, writing out of Columbia, teaches that: "God the preeminently free being, forms a union with another free being, putting into that person's hands a world to transform and society to build, a human work that needs no unreal religious justifications" (9:104). Again, man is "born free," can rise to a partnership with God who is by nature "free," without concern about "unreal" notions like a Fall and vicarious redemption!

First doctrinal victim, then, which LT sacrifices to its Marxist commitment: the Fall.

2. Second Doctrinal Victim: Death as Penalty upon the Fall

But what, then, of the penalty which God threatened upon man's disobedience: "You shall surely die!"

Does not that gloomy witness to inherent human defect continue to haunt us? The Fall may be dropped from LT's version of the Bible, but death is not so easily dropped from the human agenda. The punishment of the depravity inherited from Adam and Eve hangs with grim finality over everyone's destiny.

Even death does not blunt LT's commitment to Marxism, however. The Liberationist is ingenious—and, like Marx, can draw limitless drafts upon the bank of the future. LT prophesies a time when death, too, will be conquered—via the Marxist dialectic!

To begin with, LT finds it natural to assume that God takes His own Word as lightly as LT does. For minds committed to materialism, the divine judgment of death never did befall erring mankind, and indeed the Genesis account of the Fall is not to be taken as historical anyway.

So José Miranda can quote with evident satisfaction German theologian Gerhard van Rad: "The threat of Gen. 2:17—'On the day you eat of that tree you shall surely die'—was simply a threat which was never fulfilled" (66:91). That this threat is recorded in a Scripture which both van Rad and LT are occasionally given to quoting as authoritative makes, in this instance, no difference. Let Genesis say what it will, it's not so! One may take van Rad's word on it! Whatever accounts for the universality of death, it is not the Fall!

So Miranda joins the speculative theologian in announcing: "The Old Testament does not teach that death is the penalty of sin" (66:91). What does it matter to LT ideology and speculative German theology, which expurgate the Bible at will, that St. Paul has a diametrically opposite view: "Therefore as sin came into the world through one man and death through sin, and so death spread to all men because all men sinned . . ." (Rom. 5:12).

Did, then, God threaten the mythical Adam and Eve with an exaggerated penalty, one which He had no intention of executing upon them—as an angry parent might foolishly menace an unruly child? And did primitive man get away, so to speak, with calling God's bluff?

Or might God, not subject to speculative manipulation and not being a materialist, have threatened, and executed, a far more frightening "death," one which would thereafter begin at birth to infect also the physical? Did not God mean by "death" an alienation from Himself, the source of all life, the true life of which that enjoyed in the body became after the Fall but a temporal, and temporary, manifestation? And did not God visit upon His erring image-bearers precisely that eternal "death" to which all physical dying now attests? So the Bible—being neither Marxist nor materialist—teaches!

Man is by inheritance St. Paul writes, "Dead in trespasses and sins" (Eph. 2:1).

The "death" which God decreed and our first parents suffered, and from which only the Second Adam can deliver us, is severance of true life at its taproot—communion with God, who alone has life in Himself. It is only the palest, most materialist, incredibly naive conception of "death" which views the divine penalty as aborted on the occasion of that primal, awesome disobedience. The sovereign God need not—probably can not—bluff!

Still more, what ultimate importance could the very concept of "liberation" have did it not denote triumph over the *eternal* "death" suffered by Adam and Eve and their progeny as a result of that fatal disobedience? What "liberation" might be secured by rebellion is at best temporal, and absolutely incommensurable with the havoc wrought by our first parents' disobedience.

Is it because LT senses this deficiency that it denies the penalty of the Fall, and wildly surmises that dialectic can destroy physical death, as we shall see?

Sound, traditional, biblical Christianity proclaims eternal victory over the "death" imposed upon man's primal disobedience. Biblical Christianity, therefore, truly *liberates!* The Christ, who through His death slew death for those who believe, is able—and He alone!—to "deliver them who through fear of death were all their lifetime subject to bondage" (Heb. 2:15). Thanks to Jesus, not to the dialectic, Paul can announce, "The last enemy that shall be destroyed is death" (I Cor. 15:26).

LT is mistaken about the nature of "death" because it is mistaken about the nature of "life"—both errors rooted in the same sacrifice to Marxism: the Bible!

The inspired Word makes clear that the "death" which befell mankind in Eden cut the umbilical cord binding man to the Source and Ground of his creation. Victims ourselves of this alienation, stumbling in the darkness of our own inherited myopia, man can know and escape his bondage to death only by accepting through faith the "life" offered in the Word by the Christ who is Himself, "the way, the truth, and the life" (John 14:6). LT seeks new life in rebellion because it has cut itself off from knowing, through revelation and by faith, what is the "death" which shrouds its own reflections in darkness.

But, having reduced "death" to materialist dimensions, LT procedes to reread the Bible accordingly:

"Cain," writes Miranda, "was the first concrete man, and human history begins" with Cain's murder of his brother Abel (Gen. 4:1-11). Once again, the biblical account is conceded to Marxist requirements, for the Bible nowhere suggests that Cain was progenitor of mankind!

What "concrete man" means, as descriptive of Cain, is that prior to Cain's appearance, the Genesis account deals only, in Miranda's words, "with man in general." How "man in general" gives birth to Cain the "concrete" is left unclear. The Bible surely knows nothing of such a miracle.

Miranda continues: "The Yahwist [which is in-term for one of the two, or more, presumed writers, or compilers, of Genesis] is not trying to write concrete history but rather is philosophizing on man in general with the help of pre-Israelite sagas" (66:92). Ingenious, these Liberationists! But really a blatant "rereading" into the text what is nowhere to be found there.

But was St. Paul, then, ignorant that the Christ came in response to Cain's rather than Adam's sin, when he discourses so tellingly on the crucial relation of the "first" to the "second" Adam in Romans 5?

What the LT ideologue intends, of course, is introducing death into history in terms that dialectical materialism can cope with—or at least be said to cope with.

Miranda eagerly seizes upon the opportunity he provides himself: "What we must reproach Marx for when he avoids the problem of death and therefore does not even glimpse the possibility of the resurrection of the dead is that he was not sufficiently dialectical" (p. 278). Death, visited upon history by Cain, has been awaiting an LT extension of Marxist dialectic for its elimination!

Contemporary Marxist Ernst Bloch happily corrects Marx's oversight: "In contrast to mechanistic materialism," Bloch asserts, "dialectics knows no nothingness predetermined beforehand and imposed by an order supposedly desired by nature" (66:280, quoted from Bloch's *Das Prinzip Hoffnung,* 1382). This murky rhetoric implies, for Miranda at least, that what dialectic doesn't "know" may therefore be denied. If dialectic is aware of no "nothingness," then death, which is "nothingness," is thus overcome. A neat dialectical trick which Miranda faults Marx for muffing, but when is death itself going to find that out?

From Bloch Miranda derives this conclusion: "The elimination of injustice in mankind will bring with it the definitive defeat of death" (66:281).

But Miranda is not through. It was Sigmund Freud, too, he says, who got the right slant on death: "What is now holding sway in the superego is, as it were, a pure culture of the death instinct," Miranda quotes Freud as writing in his *The Ego And The Id.* Here Miranda scents a clue, and quickly adds, "As is well known, in the superego there is all of human civilization with its structures, its taboos, its laws, its ideologies" (66:281). Death has the last word because, a la Freud, modernity is obsessed with its own death wish! That is all. And what Freud calls the "superego," Miranda says, "is the same human civilization which Paul calls 'cosmos' or 'eon' . . ." (66:281). Paul was, without knowing it, an early Freudian.

What then?

Simple! Let violent hands, steeled to their wreckage by Marxist-LT ideology, bring this repressive civilization to its end, and, with it death! Pshaw! Isn't it obvious that, "Repression is oppression and it is injustice. And death is the extreme form of repression." Out with repression, down with oppression, and . . . exit death!

Does not Freud postulate, "It may be, however, that this belief in the internal necessity of dying is only another of those illusions which we have created" (in his *Beyond The Pleasure Principle*)?

Thus encouraged by Bloch and Freud, Miranda is ready to announce his own version of liberation from death: "All these observations point in this direction: In a world in which there is no longer oppression or enmity or mistrust or injustice, death too will disappear" (66:282). Something of a momentous conclusion to hang upon "all these [three] observations!"

Why was Marx blind to so breathtaking a consummation?

We will let Miranda inform us: "I repeat: When Marx avoids the problem of death and therefore does not even glimpse the possibility of resurrection, it is not precisely his lack of faith in God but rather insufficient dialectics for which we must reproach him" (66:279).

Who can believe all this can, no doubt, believe anything!

But Miranda is not alone.

"Like other traditional Christian themes," writes Fierro, "the resurrection is being subjected to hermeneutic recasting in current political theology" (33:295). As a "theme," death may no doubt be cast and recast with every change of ideological scenery. Alas, as a fact it stubbornly stalks us all, despite Bloch, Freud, Miranda & Co.

What LT ignores, being, like its Marxist predecessor, thoroughly materialist, is that any "death" over which dialectic might dream of winning a victory is not the spiritual death befallen mankind through

Adam and Eve. Only God in Christ triumphs over that! The glory, mystery and power which the Bible celebrates in the physical resurrection of Jesus, and foretastes for all the faithful in the last chapters of the book of Revelation and elsewhere can no more be confined to Freudian or Marxist categories than heaven can be described as the classless society!

Miranda is, or ought to be, incontrovertibly instructive. By driving LT to ultimate absurdity, he warns those about to set foot upon its illusive path to stop, look, listen and turn elsewhere.

The Communist states write "human depravity" in letters large enough for the world to see. A work like Miranda's writes "inherited blindness" in words perverse enough for all but the self-deluded to perceive. Inherited depravity blinds first of all those who deny its reality. Of such St. Paul warns the Thessalonians, "God sends upon them a strong delusion, to make them believe what is false, so that all may be condemned who did not believe the truth but had pleasure in unrighteousness" (II Thess. 2:11).

Second doctrinal victim, then, which LT sacrifices to its Marxist commitment: death as penalty upon the Fall.

3. Third Doctrinal Victim: God the First Marxist

LT obscures its rejection of the Fall by stepping quickly from God the Creator to God the author of class struggle—thus making Him the original Marxist.

"Yahweh, the God of the Bible," Enzo Gatti announces, "enters on the stage of history as a revolutionary, liberating force. In the first phase of his activity, he frees Israel from Egyptian domination; in the second (still limited to the Israelite people), he frees the exploited from the exploiter; in the third (the last great historical experience of Israel), he once more delivers his people, this time from Babylonian oppression" (37:ix). Not once, it appears, in all this recital of divine intervention does it occur to this Liberationist that in no instance did Yahweh choose to incite Israel to liberate herself through the kind of violent rebellion which LT advocates. Israel is not a model for the poor who "save" themelves via rebellion; Israel is model for the innately depraved who need divine deliverance through God's, not their own, effort.

The Exodus is touted over and again by Liberationists of all stripes to instance God's preference for the rebel who takes history by the forelock and forges his own redemption through violent opposition to the status quo. But Israel forged no such liberation for herself. Nor does the God of the Bible ever convert His people into rebels. One rebellion—that in the Garden—did damage enough!

What the Creator, as LT describes Him, wanted, in consonance with Marxist dialectic, was to kick off the class struggle! Marx composed the tune to which history has danced from the beginning—and God wanted it so!

Gatti has it like this: "The Bible thus shows us that Yahweh's first involvement with his people is involvement in an act of liberation that takes them from Egypt to the promised land by way of the desert" (37:10).

Is that how the Bible tells it? Was God's "first involvement" with Israel effected in Egypt? Israel surely did not think so. Did it not trace its history back to the Patriarchs, its very name back to Jacob, and reckon its favored status in terms already vouchsafed by God to Abraham, recipient of the promises and "the father of the faithful?" And did not, too, the wilderness road lead out of Egypt to Sinai and the Law? And was the Law not the very backbone of Israel's "self-understanding," as the jargon goes? This is indeed Moses' view in the great oration titled Deuteronomy. But not Gatti's! All he knows is that "The God of the Exodus creates for the human community the category of power, newness, freedom from limitations. Thanks to him creation and history become open-ended realities" (37:29). So the imagination is pitted against the biblical record, and the result called "theological reflection!"

Gustavo Gutierrez baptizes God a Marxist with a fanciful formula: "The creation of the world initiates history, the human struggle, and the salvific adventure of Yahweh" (43:154). Marx would have relished the dramatic touch—the world a stage, his ideology the script, mankind already in class struggle, and the Director coming along on a "salvific adventure!"

Gutierrez adds, "Creation is presented in the Bible, not as a stage previous to salvation, but as part of the salvific process." And again, "The Bible establishes a close link between creation and salvation. But the link is based on the historical and liberating experience of the Exodus" (43:153).

But the "link between creation and salvation" forged by the Bible is not the Exodus but the Word Christ, agent of creation and of re-creation by faith. And the Christ had to undertake His self-sacrificial obligation because between the creation and the Exodus was, among other things, the Fall! The Liberationist is, therefore, quite mistaken in urging that "creation and liberation from Egypt are but one salvific act" (p. 155), a schema useful to ideology but utterly foreign to the Bible.

But if God did intend "salvific" action via "struggle" from the moment of creation, then it would be God who initiated the class struggle. God is, as we were saying, for LT the first Marxist.

Hugo Assmann is sweepingly unequivocal: "In biblical exegesis, political theology lays the stress once again on the meaning of the Exodus as the original principle on which the whole biblical concept of God and faith is based . . ." (5:35). Stripped of his ideological commitment, Assmann verges on the correct, for Exodus does signalize as no other biblical event man's total incapacity for self-redemption—it was God, and God alone, who called His "son" out of Egypt (Matt. 2:15; Ex. 4:22); and it was God, and God alone, Moses says, not our rebellion, who "brought us out of Egypt with a mighty hand and outstretched arm, with great terror, with signs and wonders" (Deut. 26: 8).

The Exodus is paradigm of man's fall into bondage in the Garden of Eden, and God's liberation of those who believe in the mighty acts of divine Incarnation, death and resurrection. But to make of the Exodus a paradigm for violent revolution en route to self-recreation is to parody and pervert the "signs and wonders" God intends His people to heed in this great and terrible demonstration of His power and judgment.

Gone from LT "exegesis" of the Exodus are Christ's own references to the symbolic miracles recorded there: 1) "As Moses lifted up the serpent in the wilderness, so must the Son of Man be lifted up . . ." (John 3:14); 2) "Your fathers ate the manna in the wilderness, and they died. This is the bread which comes down from heaven, that a man may eat of it and not die" (John 6:49-50); 3) with obvious reference to the water which flowed out of the rock in the wilderness (which Paul says "was Christ"—I Cor. 10:4), Jesus cries, "If anyone thirst let him come to me and drink" (John 7:38). The Exodus is an infinitely suggestive paradigm of the Christian life. How much more in accord with "solid" traditional exegesis, and how much more useful to the Latin American poor and rich alike, would be an exposition of what Exodus really has to teach us rather than Miranda's serpentine manipulation of the Bible into an ephemeral ally of Karl Marx!

Alfredo Fierro claims an insight into the meaning of the Exodus which the inspiring Spirit neglected to convey: "The fact that the biblical authors might not have taken account of the subversive political significance of the flight from Egypt is not a crushing blow"—we recall the writer who says that what the New Testament omits "doesn't matter!"

"The crucial point is that from the way they relate the event this subversive political significance seems to be clear and obvious. It flows from the very nature of the event itself, whether those who reported the event in the Bible were aware of it or not. The Exodus from Egypt was a political act, clearly bearing the stamp of resistance and rebellion. And if an action of that sort lies at the very origin of biblical tradition, then on that score there is justification for an Exodus theology and its prolongations in a theology of liberation" (33:147). How to have it both ways: if the Bible lamentably neglects to provide the interpretation which LT needs, provide that interpretation by fiat! Just too bad those inspired reporters didn't catch on!

What any reader of the Bible, not victimized by ideological myopia, can readily see, however, is that the Israelites cowering on the far side of the Red Sea, which had just this moment opened as by miracle to give them passage, bore no resemblance to a force stamped with the character of "resistance and rebellion." Their whimpering does not cease until the same God whose arm liberated them closes the sea over the chariots they never even met, let alone bested, in violent conflict.

To make some disciplined, rebel force, fresh from victory over the hosts of Pharoah under the generalship of the Lord, out of the Israel which staggered out of Egypt and complained its way across the desert, only to freeze with fear when told that Palestinian warriors were too tall for them, is to beggar exaggeration. The Exodus reflects human impotence. The biblical account does not claim otherwise, because otherwise it was not! The rude description voiced by Moses in Deuteronomy of Israel's miniscule political importance and total incompetence to save herself is echoed and re-echoed by the Psalmists who celebrate her rescue by God's, not man's, strong arm!

Look at the Exodus, freed of ideological lenses, and be glad—if you count yourself unskilled at self-liberation! God does it all!

"Yahweh is presented as creator," Miranda holds, "to give importance to his intervention on behalf of justice. . . . As van Rad has pointed out, Genesis is the prologue, the prehistory, the preparation for the essential fact: the liberation of the slaves from Egypt" (p. 78). In a word, man was created emmeshed in the toils of class division just so God could demonstrate His sympathy for Marxist perspectives and Liberation ideology!

Marx never had it better—nor further from biblical revelation.

Third doctrinal victim sacrificed to Marxism: God the first Marxist!

4. Fourth Doctrinal Victim: Jesus the Author of Subversion

Like the Father, so the Son—in LT "theological reflection."

If God institutes class struggle, Jesus carries it through to successful rebellion.

After saying that "the God of Israel is a God of freedom who challenges every form of human slavery," Gatti goes on to say, "These characteristics, which are already evident in the pages of the Old Testament, become fully clear in Christ, who is God's definitive Word of salvation to mankind" (37:ix).

What is it that becomes "fully clear in Christ?"

Reading the Old Testament in the light of the "Christ-event," Gatti explains, "We find in it a subversive message of liberation which addresses itself to the condition of the poor and oppressed of every age" (37:6).

Is that, we ask, how Jesus Himself read the Old Testament? Where do the Evangelists say so? When did Christ ever translate the "as it is written" which governed His life, into an Old Testament call for salvation of the poor through rebellion?

This does not keep Gatti from declaring, "In Christ the God of the Exodus and of freedom manifests himself in a definitive way. He wages war upon the forces of oppression, not now in favor of a particular people from a particular stock and cultural world, but in favor of all (individuals or groups, whatever their origin) who are oppressed and in any need and who seek freedom" (37:43). If God is the first Marxist, His Son is the first rebel!

"If my kingship were of this world," Jesus says to Pilate, "my servants would fight . . . but my kingship is not of this world" (John 18:36)—not, that is, of the stuff that ideology fashions! "Do you think," Christ tells Peter, who has unsheathed his sword, "that I cannot appeal to my Father, and he will at once send me more than twelve legions of angels? But how then should the scriptures be fulfilled that it must be so" (Matt. 26:53-54)?

Of a Scriptures that must be fulfilled, LT knows little. Of a Christ going to vicarious death in preference to promoting violent rebellion, LT seems to know less.

That absence of biblical and traditional support for LT theorizing is put plainly enough by Alfredo Fierri: "Only great naivete or some sort of dogmatic prejudice could prompt one to think that the aforecited formulas of liberation Christology and other similar current Christologies mean the same as the formulas of Chalcedon or the New Testament" (33:175). But by confessedly lacking the authentication of both New Testament and, in Vidales' words, "the most solid and sound tradition of Christian theology," with what authority, then, do Liberation theories come? Speaking of the "naiev," how great a "naiveté" is it that adopts Christological theses solely on the assertion of ideologists who make them?

Fierri quotes one, Giuseppe Vaccari, who presumes upon just such naiveté: "As a universal figure belonging to all human beings, Christ cannot be recovered with the instruments of traditional theology and the one-track interpretational guidelines that tend to flesh him out in an acritical and mythical milieu. We must go back behind the mediating influences of Greek and Latin culture, fleshing out his figure by somehow recovering his human actions" (33:181, quoting from *Teologia della rivoluzione*). By "somehow recovering . . . ?" And how is that?

It is natural that so chimerical a Jesus should Himself fall under LT judgment: "The decision to focus on Jesus alone and opt for him is justified in so far," Fierro posits, "as that particular man proves to be capable of generating a liberation praxis that lasts down through the centuries and continues on in the future" (33:399).

"That particular man"—no more, no less! The LT "Jesus" had better produce to LT specifications, or else!

Fierro leaves no doubt about it: "The harsh judgment of Vaccari is correct in the last analysis: 'If man is not liberated, Christ has not risen' " (33:399, quoting from same title)! "In the last analysis" LT adopts Marxist standards! That we have been seeing all along.

Leonardo Boff complains that in what he calls "traditional" interpretations, "Christ's death is detached from the rest of his life and begins to possess a salvific meaning of its own. In such a case the historical dimension of Jesus' death is lost for the most part. We no longer see it as the consequence of his own attitudes and the outcome of a judicial process" (39:116-17).

To avert this penchant for misunderstanding, Boff teaches that Christ's death "was not imposed from without by any divine decree" (39:117).

What might Boff make, then, if he took it seriously, of Christ's own conviction that He went to His death that the "Scripture be fulfilled"—as quoted above. Or of the whole New Testament understanding of the crucifixion as enunciated by Peter at Pentecost: "This Jesus, delivered up according to the definite plan and foreknowledge of God, you crucified and killed by the hands of lawless men" (Acts 2:23).

The choice spells out itself:

Leonardo Boff: "not imposed from without by any divine decree!"

St. Peter: "delivered up according to the definite plan and foreknowledge of God!"

LT *or* the Bible?

LT prefers Marx. And you, reader?

Boff goes on to say that Christ's "liberative project grew out of a profound personal experience of God as the absolute sense of all history . . ." but that "Jesus did not experience God as the God of the

Mosaic law, a God making clear distinctions between the good and the wicked, the just and unjust. His experience is with a good God who loves and pardons people . . ." (39:121).

Yes, God *loves!* Enough to give His Son to the Cross (John 3:16). And yes, God pardons: "When I see the blood, I will pass over you" (Ex. 12:13, and Heb. 11:28)! And *this* God is, indeed, "good." Just because He is, no sentimental by-pass of sin, a la Boff, is even thinkable.

As to making "clear distinctions between good and evil," it is Jesus Himself who, in His Father's name, more sharply distinguishes the destiny of the good from that of the evil, and dilates more vividly on the punishments of hell, than any other figure in the Bible.

Fourth doctrinal victim, then, sacrificed to Marxism: Jesus becomes the author of subversion!

5. Fifth Doctrinal Victim: The Atonement

At the heart of Marxism/LT is rebellion.

At the heart of the Gospel is the atoning death of Christ.

St. John hears the song of the redeemed, echoing in heaven: "Worthy art thou," sing the elders representing the Church, "for thou wast slain and by thy blood didst ransom men for God from every tribe and tongue and people and nation, and hast made them a kingdom and priests to our God, and they shall reign on earth" (Rev. 5:9-10).

And St. Paul: "Christ . . . gave himself for us, that he might redeem us from all iniquity" (Titus 2:14).

If Christ's redemptive death and glorious resurrection be not what the Incarnation is all about, then, "Let us eat and drink," St. Paul writes, "for tomorrow we die" (I Cor. 15:32). But if, on the contrary, as is the case, God "did not spare his own Son but gave him up for us all . . , then we are more than conquerors through him who loved us" (Rom. 8:32, 37).

Central to Christianity is the doctrine of the Atonement, foreshadowed by the Passover in Egypt, and the ensuing ceremonies of Israel, realized in the life and death and resurrection of Jesus, and ours by a faith working through obedience (Rom. 1:5).

And here we meet again the crucial clash between Christianity and Marxism—with LT opting for Marxism: either man liberates himself via rebellion, according to Marx; or God liberates those who believe through Jesus Christ, according to the Scriptures.

True to its Marxist commitments, LT "moves away" from the Atonement.

Hugo Assmann puts it plainly: "Our Christological tracts have moved from the individual Christ to the total Christ; from Christ *in se* to the Christ 'in Christians'; and, more timidly and gradually, from the bygone Christ to a Christ and his power operating in the full dimensions of history and here and now today" (39:124).

No doubt LT "Christological tracts" have indeed moved from the Christ of the Scriptures to the Christ "in Christians." We have, indeed, already met a Liberationist who thinks of himself as re-incarnating the "Christ-event." But such a moving is "away" from the Christ of the Scriptures and in the direction of Marxism.

And why, in passing, should any theology come "timidly and gradually" to a conception of Christ as "here and now today?" Did not the Christ of the Scriptures plainly say, "Lo, I am with you always, to the close of the age" (Matt. 28:20)? But the Christ who said that, of course, is not dispersed "in Christians," but seated on the right hand of His Father in heaven (Col. 3:1), who has given Him "all authority in heaven and on earth" (Matt. 28:18)—characteristics that cannot be divided up among "Christians" to suit LT convenience!

The LT Christ, even though only found "in Christians" has, Assmann says, an LT characteristic: "Christ's power is necessarily operative in a certain well-defined direction. It is on the side of the oppressed and against their oppressors" (39:146).

That "well-defined direction" is, of course, laid out by Marxism and imposed upon a Bible where it is nowhere to be found. As we have already observed, according to the Bible, "Christ Jesus came into the world to save sinners" (I Tim. 1:15), not via rebellion but via the Cross—a salvation not attained through rebellion but through faith. Much as LT would like to focus the "direction" taken by the Atonement according to its Marxist formulae, the Bible drags its feet. It *is* sinners, not a rebel proletariat, that the Christ comes with "well-defined" determination to save.

Gutierrez tells us, "The God who makes the cosmos is the same God who leads Israel from alienation to liberation . . . The work of Christ is part of this movement and brings it to complete fulfillment . . . The work of Christ is a new creation . . . Consequently, when we assert that man fulfills himself by continuing the work of creation by means of his labor, we are saying that he places himself, by this very fact, within an all-embracing salvific process. To work, to transform this world, is to become a man and to build the human community; it is also to save" (43:158-59).

"To work, to transform . . . is also to save!" The Bible has it just the other way around: being re-*new*-ed in Christ man is then empowered by the Spirit to transform himself and his community. It is, thus, quite unbiblical to say, as Gutierrez does, "The life and preaching of Jesus postulate the unceasing search for a new kind of man in a qualitatively different society" (43:231)—for this is but another way of saying that Marx and Jesus pursued the same end: a new kind of man self-made through a new society.

This cooperative effort is facilitated by the fact that, according to Gutierrez, "Christ is not a private individual. . . . We find the Lord in our encounters with men, especially the poor, marginated, and exploited ones" (43:201-02).

Gutierrez hails joint Marxist/LT social maneuvers with a rhetorical flourish: "There is," he affirms, "only one history—a 'Christo-finalized' history" (43:153). This being so, whoever continues "the work of creation by means of his labor"—be he Christian or Marxist!—places himself "within an all-embracing salvific process!"

Whatever a "Christo-finalized" history may be, one thing is evident: in the Bible as reread in LT, the Christ is "in" the exploited and with them takes to the streets, waving a red flag and shouting Marxist slogans. The awesome import of Calvary, like the Fall which occasioned it, is sacrificed to Marxism, the transaction obscured with a flourish of verbal trumpets: a "Christo-finalized history!"

For José Comblin, "Freedom is the main feature and the reason of Christ's nature and action" (18:124), thus neatly fashioning a Comrade Jesus whose "action" will promote Marxist rebellion.

For LT has a freedom in view which man attains for himself, and by violence: "Liberty will not be a tranquil evolution overcoming established domination and slavery by means of a quiet explanation of the truth."

Why not? Because, "history is still sin and domination, but with the advent of the Spirit it has also becomes struggle against sin and domination, the beginning of liberty and truth" (18:159).

Step by inexorable step the "freedom" which Christ brings must be won through "struggle" which takes on, more and more, the lineaments of Marxist rebellion: "Citizens must make themselves free or they will never become free" (18:162).

Christ's gift has become man's attainment, with Christ the model revolutionary: "Jesus himself stood up against Jewish and Roman power in a radical way only after several years of preaching" (18:173); and with Him as model, "freedom has to be conquered by each person in an ongoing struggle against state and power" (18:193).

"So a real, ongoing conflict between the calling for freedom and the structure of a nation-state cannot be avoided" (18:194).

Christ the full-fledged, pre-Marxist subversive emerges at last: "The strategy of liberation is to support all true movements for the liberation of people by undertaking their struggles and sufferings, their slavery and hope, their rebellion and martyrdom. . . . It recognizes Christ's salvation in the popular movements" (18:215).

The LT "Christ" is perverted into the servant of Marxism, ready to shoulder arms with the "workers of the world." If anyone doubts this, listen to Hugo Assmann:

"The theology of liberation, as an effective process of critical reflection on historical practice, will have to go back to the theology of the cross. It will also have to strip it of the alienating mystifications that have accrued to it. The most obvious of these would seem to be the 'theory of satisfaction', pushed to the extreme of the scapegoat who died for those who project on to him their own cowardice and failure to rise to the challenge of their historical reponsibilities; another is the theory of the 'reconciler' who pacifies everything and tries to avoid any sort of conflict. It will have to give back to the man Jesus his full integrity as a human being, and give his death the historical and political meaning that in fact it possessed" (5:86).

Which is more offensive in this effusion, its condescension or its arrogance? Which is the more astonishng, the contemptuous dismissal of the Church's understanding of the Atonement, or the total subordination of Jesus Christ to Marxist requirements?

What LT calls "the theory of satisfaction" and would "strip" from the "theology of the cross" is sound and solid doctrine embedded in the Bible from Genesis to the New Testament—and taught by the Church from its beginnings: "God was in Christ reconciling the world the world to himself, not counting their trespasses against them . . ." (II Cor. 5:19).

And what has *this* Christ in common with a fiction "who pacifies everything and tries to avoid any sort of conflict"? The Christ of the Bible, quite to the contrary, says plainly enough for even a Liberationist to hear, if he will: "I have not come to bring peace, but a sword" (Matt. 10:34). Where, apart from his Marxist myopia, can a Liberation Theologian see his kind of Christ in the Jesus of the Bible?

The LT intent, however, appears here once more: Christ must be adapted to Marxist dynamics, and must produce visible fruit in rebellion, if He is to be acknowledged at all. In a word: serve Marx or sign out!

And what comment can be made on the travesty of "those who project on to him their own cowardice and failure . . ."? Really!

Among the heroes of history have been the saints who went to torture and death, after having laid their cowardice on His shoulders, and at His bidding charged their failures to His account.

Fifth doctrinal victim, then, sacrificed to Marxism: the Atonement!

6. Sixth Doctrinal Victim: Conversion

Liberation Theology concedes to its Marxist commitments the Christian concept of conversion.

Conversion denotes change. The change in view is from a life of inherited servitude to the Devil to a life of God-given liberation through obedience, by faith, to the Word of God.

It must be noted that Christian conversion takes off from repentance. Repentance is the first fruit of faith.

It is striking, when one once becomes sensitive to it, how uniformly New Testament preaching opens with "Repent!"

John the Baptist, forerunner of the Christ, comes demanding repentance: "In those days came John the Baptist, preaching in the wilderness of Judea, 'Repent, for the kingdom of heaven is at hand' " (Matt. 3:2). That is, repudiate your allegiance to the Kingdom of Darkness and claim citizenship in the Kingdom of Light!

So, too, the Christ: "Now after John was arrested, Jesus came into Galilee, preaching the gospel of God, and saying, 'The time is fulfilled, and the kingdom of God is at hand; repent, and believe the gospel' " (Mark 1:14-15). Turn, that is, from ideology to Truth!

The first disciples, sent out at their Lord's command: "So they went out and preached that all men should repent" (Mark 6:12). "*All* men . . . !"

The reader can ascertain for himself that "Repent" prefixed the preaching of St. Peter on Pentecost (Acts 2:37-38), was on the lips of St. Paul at Athens (Acts 18:30) and characterizes Paul's general account of his ministry before King Agrippa and Festus (Acts 26:19-20). Finally, it is from heaven itself that St. John hears the risen Christ calling, "Be zealous and repent" (Rev. 3:19)!

The force of "repent" is this: get yourself a new Master! the right Master! the only real Master! the God who made you, redeems you, and will infuse your will with the commitment to do His will! Repent!

Repent: foreswear allegiance to self, to fad, to ideology—seductions used by the Devil to hold us in Egyptian bondage under the guise of freedom.

Yes, repent! But, of course, repentance presumes inherited bondage, depravity innate from birth, in short: the Fall!

And, over the threshhold of repentance, "conversion" means entrance upon the Kingdom of God by acknowledging Him as Master and His Law as guide to life. Conversion denotes a naturalization, a resumption of citizenship lost in Adam. Conversion is change, from the slavery of license to the liberty of obedience. Conversion commonly leads to active participation in the Church where God's will is taught and obedience to it encouraged and disciplined.

The call to repentance is universal. It excludes no one, not even ideologists and theologians! It knows no class boundaries, because bondage to God's Adversary knows none.

"All men," St. Paul teaches, "are under the power of sin," as the Psalmist says, "None is righteous, no, not one; All have turned aside, together they have gone wrong; no one does good, not even one" (Rom. 3:9-12; quoting Ps. 14:1-3). The condemnation is without exception; it includes the bourgeoisie, the proletariat, the Marxist, the Liberation Theologian and all the rest of us!

This is why, obviously, true spokesmen for the Lord call upon "all men to repent!"

And the sobering implication ought to be unmistakable: the unrepentant are crippled by the heritage which only repentance sloughs off!

There is something to repent of, something which corrupts the unrepentant, or the Lord and all His disciples would not begin their preaching there. That something is, indeed, so subtle that only the first step of faith perceives it: man is innately incapable of redeeming himself, and the master to whom he is born enslaved has only illusion to offer! Repent!

Repent! Convert your linguistic currency of the land of the shadow into the linguistic currency of the land of everlasting light!

But, having rejected the Fall, both Marxism and LT want to know nothing of course about repentance, least of all their own need of it!

What LT says of "conversion" is never prefixed by "Repent!" and comes couched in Marxist language and bound by Marxist parameters.

Let us ask LT: what is "conversion?"

Gutierrez answers: "To be converted is to commit oneself to the process of the liberation of the poor and oppressed, to commit oneself lucidly, realistically, and concretely. It means to commit oneself not only generously, but also with an analysis of the situation and a strategy of action" (43:205).

Quite a different notion of "conversion" than that of the Bible and the Church! And it happens that we know well whose "analysis" and whose "strategy of action" he has in mind: Marx's!

But the reader may reflect on this: if repentance is as indispensable to true conversion as the Bible represents it, then commitment to unrepentant rebellion cannot be, all things considered, so "lucid," so "realistic," and so "concrete" as LT deludes itself into believing.

Gutierrez has more to say about conversion: "Conversion means a radical transformation of ourselves; it means thinking, feeling, and living as Christ—present in the exploited and alienated man" (43:205)! This is so grotesquely at odds with the Scriptures as to beggar comment.

"Theology both derives from and leads to conversion," Luis del Valle writes. "Conversion is here understood as a real commitment to, and involvement in, society. Society must be changed . . ." (39:83).

Marx was as much a genuine convert (or as little a genuine convert), by this definition, as is the Liberationist.

Segundo Galilea gives "conversion" an ideological twist: "In liberation terms 'sinners' are the exploiters and those who act unjustly. A message of liberation is addressed to them also, though in different terms. They must undergo conversion and become poor, abetting the liberation of the poor rather than hindering it" (43:179). LT commends "conversion" only to those on its hit list.

" 'Conversion,' " says Alfredo Fierro, "is the Christian name for 'revolution' . . . liberating revolution in the conversion of societies" (33:235).

LT has a pejorative term for individual repentance. It is called "'moralism," which is, Fierro says, quoting Marx, "impotence in action."

Taking his cue from Marx, Fierro concludes that New Testament preaching was in error: "The moralism of individual conversion now appears as a great historical mistake committed by Christians" (33:234).

Hugo Assmann proclaims his myopia thus: "Yet the Bible is full of this: conversion, whether individual or societal, implies assumption of conflict" (5:98)—the kind of class struggle conflict which Marx and LT have in view. For Assmann, "conversion" is to ideology rather than to Christ and Kingdom.

Sixth LT doctrinal victim sacrificed to Marxism: the concept of conversion.

7. Seventh Doctrinal Victim: Love

"Love" is a uniquely Christian plenitude. "God so loved the world," St. John says, "that he gave his only Son, that whoever believes in him should not perish but have eternal life" (John 3:16)—one of the most familiar texts in the Bible. God thus sets the pattern. Love gives! Divine love gives far beyond our capacity to measure or understand.

St. Paul pens a familiar hymn extolling the scope of love in the thirteenth chapter of his first letter to Corinth.

St. John devotes much of three epistles to the delineation of Christian love, and in one of them defines God Himself as love (I John 4:8).

Christian love is distinguished in the Scriptures from desire and the lust to possess, characteristics of romantic love. Christian love is also set apart from the affection prevailing among friends.

Christian love is unique, modeled by the total devotion of the Christ who gave His life for His Church and by the Father who thus gave His Son to the Cross. "But God shows his love for us," St. Paul says, "in that while we were yet sinners Christ died for us" (Rom. 5:8). Christian love, Paul says, "bears all things, believes all things, hopes all things, endures all things. Love never ends" (I Cor. 13:7-8).

How, then, does LT deal with this sublime reality, the love God has for those who are "yet sinners?" Does the Liberationist corrupt this Christian truth too?

He does!

Liberation Theology fits the sublime biblical conception of love with Marxist blinders. LT "love" but thinly cloaks the lust for revenge, the hatred of which Guevara speaks, and the passion for an ultimate cataclysm which would bring LT/Marxists to political power.

Too strong a charge?

Not at all!

Hear Hugo Assmann: "We need to get rid of falsely conciliatory disfigurements of Christian thought and behavior, and to release the rebel, negative and conflictive energies of love so as to see it in action as conflict in history: to design models of Christian love that are also models of liberating struggle" (5:98). In a word, LT would refashion "love" into an instrument of Marxist rebellion—and no longer, then, Christian love!

Jean Cardonnel does it this way: "If I am to live the great commandment of love and treat the wealthy landowners as brothers, I must engage in the struggle that will dispossess them" (33:232). Happily the Christ's love for sinners takes on other dimensions! But for *this* Liberationist love must take on Marxist lineaments if he is to practice it! "There is," he adds, "no more forceful gesture of love for one's enemies than the one that breaks down their privileged elitist situation and ushers them into the immense joy of a shared common condition" (33:232). Is this meant to be irony or humor?

Jules Girardi: "One must love all, but not all in the same way. One loves the oppressed by liberating them from their misery; one loves the oppressors by liberating them from their sinfulness" (33:191). Once again, "love" warped to fit Marxist categories. But how, on biblical terms, could anyone, even a Liberation Theologian, himself heir to the bondage of depravity, "liberate" either oppressor or oppressed from their "sinfulness?"

Paulo Freire maintains, "Authentic revolutionaries must come to see their revolution as an act of love, since it is a creative, humanizing activity" (33:231-32). Just how "creative" and "humanizing" a revolutionary act of love can be is explained by Girardi: "Of course it is terrible to have to kill for the sake of love, but it may prove to be necessary" (33:232). At least the facade is stripped away from Freire's euphemisms.

It is, of course, Marxism and not "love" that masquerades killing as "necessary," but for Marx himself it must be said that he never indulged in such deception. That he left to those calling themselves "theologians!"

José Comblin gives this Marxist twist to love: "The service of love is not a subordination to the aspirations or desires of the neighbor, but a service to liberating the neighbor from his or her own slavery" (5:148).

In a word, LT mints the central Christian concept of "love" into thirty pieces of silver stamped out by Marxist dies.

Seventh doctrinal victim sacrificed to Marxism: the concept of love!

8. Eighth Doctrinal Victim: *Praxis*

The term "praxis" has acquired a special status in Liberation "theological reflection," as it has in Marxist ideology.

It is only out of involvement in revolutionary *praxis,* as LT tells it, that sound "reflection" can emerge. In short, only those bound to Marxist commitments can—ironically enough—be theologians!

In common parlance, "praxis" means "practice." The Bible calls it "works."

St. James puts the importance of praxis succinctly: "Faith without works is dead" (Jas. 2:20). Belief without practice is barren.

This is an elemental and cherished Christian doctrine. Biblical enunciation of it appears throughout the Scriptures.

But, again, LT rejects the biblical concept in favor of the Marxist.

For the Bible, practice follows upon faith. Practice certifies faith. While faith itself comes from the Word of God preached: "So faith comes from what is heard, and what is heard comes by the preaching of Christ" (Rom. 10:17).

What flows from faith is, naturally, defined by faith. The practice which the Bible has in view is governed by the Bible itself.

But the praxis which LT has in view is governed by the word of Marx!

What kind of praxis does the Bible have in view? What works testify to a faith that is very much alive?

Jesus says, "If you love me, you will keep my commandments" (John 14:15). The practice which demonstrates the presence of a true faith is a life lived in devotion to the Lord's commandments.

Christ Himself spells out the kind of praxis which leads to true liberation: "If you continue in my word, you are truly my disciples, and you will know the truth, and the truth will make you free" (John 8:31).

No room, because no need, for ideology.

From the divine perspective, developed by St. Augustine in his *City Of God,* the world falls daily into two kingdoms identified by the praxis of two antithetical loyalties: the one practised by citizens who seek to keep the Lord's Word; and the other practised by citizens who obey the word of another, His Adversary the Devil. So it has been from that morning in the Garden of Eden. And just because it is so, all secularisms banish that Garden and its calamatous Fall from their systems—and so does LT!

But there is but one praxis required by, and pleasing to, the Lord: "If you continue in my word . . ."—continue, that is, doing My will.

It is the Christ, not we, nor any amount of "theological reflection" or Marxist ideology, who determines what kind of praxis demonstrates a true, believing discipleship, His way to genuine liberation!

Moreover, the task of the Church, assigned by the Lord in the so-called Great Commission, comes to focus on just this understanding of praxis: "Go therefore and make disciples of all nations, baptizing them in the name of the Father and of the Son and of the Holy Spirit, teaching them to do all that I have commanded you; and lo, I am with you always, to the close of the age" (Matt. 28:19-20).

No hint of ideology, rebellion, speculation, theological reflection: "all" that "I" have commanded!

And where shall His commands be heard?

Out of the Bible, of course!

The Lord Himself sets two alternatives: 1) "He who has my commandments and keeps them, he it is who loves me; and he who loves me will be loved by my Father, and I will love him and manifest myself to him," or, 2) "He who does not love me does not keep my words" (John 14:21, 24).

True love leads to true praxis. Both are defined by the Scriptures as obedience to His commandments, as revealed by His Word and taught in His Church! LT declaims on quite another conception of praxis, one that accords with its Marxist commitment rather than with the Bible.

"Praxis is not just a consequence of faith," writes Alfredo Fierro, and so places himself at once at odds with the Bible.

"Rather, it is intrinsic to the faith as a factor that sustains and determines its meaning" (33:75). Further at odds with the Bible, then. For LT it is man's behavior which "determines" the content of his faith, rather than the preaching of the Word which structures a faith validated by the character of his behavior.

For LT, St. James would have profited by some acquaintance with Karl Marx! It is an acquaintance which LT boasts of: "Like 'theory' in Marxist thinking, this theology is essentially bound up with praxis insofar as praxis serves as a principle of knowledge and foundation," Fierro goes on to say. "It is praxis, in other words, that provides theology with its point of origin and its legitimation" (33:107). And the praxis which LT promotes is, of course, Marxist.

Raul Vidales insists, "Liberation theology begins with concrete experience of faith as a liberation praxis" (43:43). A "liberation praxis" means, of course, liberation via Marxist rebellion. It is such praxis, Gutierrez maintains, "which becomes the matrix of a new type of theological reflection" (43:16).

But not only "new;" also exclusive: "This task of trying to comprehend the faith can be undertaken only [!] from the starting-point of real-life praxis in history, where human beings fight in order to live as human beings" (43:19).

Assmann pushes the priority of praxis, as LT defines it, to its ultimate and exclusive conclusion: "The central importance of practice as the starting-point for the theology of liberation . . . has led to a terminology in which the task of transforming the world is so intimately linked to interpretation of the world, that the latter is seen to be impossible [!] without the former" (5:74). Go Marx with LT, or go nowhere!

Or, in the words of Rubem Alves, "Truth is the name given by the historical community to those actions which were, are, and will be effective for the liberation of man" (5:76)—actions, it need hardly be recalled, as governed by Marxist ideology. Truth is Marxist, period!

Or, as Assmann goes on to say, theologians "had to participate in the process of liberation in order to find the material on which their theological thinking should be based" (5:82). Once again: take our way, or muck about in the delusion of yours!

The priority of revolutionary praxis as source of truth is not, of course, the independent discovery of Liberation Theology. It is simple Marxism.

"Marx's critical theory," writes Joseph Petulla, "begins with his philosophy of praxis . . . he is simply saying that critical theory is found in the activity of men" (74:22). Taking practice as the *source* of truth is Marxist, and diametrically antithetical to the teaching of the Bible!

For the Bible: obedient practice demonstrates belief in revealed Truth.

For Marx: praxis is the source of truth.

"*Praxis,*" says Richard J. Bernstein in his *Praxis And Action,* "is the central concept of Marx's outlook . . ." (8:13).

LT chooses the way of Marx, not that of the Bible!

LT's eighth sacrifice to Marxism, then: the concept of praxis.

9. LT's Ninth Victim: The Church

The risen Lord acts in history through His Church.

That is why the Bible describes the Church as the Lord's body: "He is the head of the body, the church," Paul writes to the Colossians; and again, "his body, that is, the church" (Col. 1:18, 24).

A more sacred name, and more dynamic concept, is not to be found.

Dietrich Bonhoeffer, German Christian martyred under Hitler, writes in his unfinished *Ethics* that "Reason, culture, humanity, tolerance and self-determination" are the "children of the Church," which in times of severe repression return "to their mother." So it was, Bonhoeffer says, under the tyranny of Nazism (11:177-78).

The roots of Western culture lie in the Church. Marxism itself is frequently discerned as an heretical perversion of the Church's most authentic aspirations for man and society.

A genuinely revolutionary slogan for our times would be, not "back to Marx," but "forward the Church!" Unfortunately, LT is correct, as was Marx, in sensing that so exciting a concept of the Church has but few advocates, even within the Church, in our times. The Church has, as LT is fond of pointing out, all too commonly identified itself with nothing in particular while parachurch groups peddle cheap leases on heavenly mansions.

And Enzo Gatti is formally correct in holding: "It is not an exaggeration to say that only a rediscovery and a concrete awareness of its own being as the mission of Christ to the world can save today's Church and reinsert it into the movement of human history" (37:45).

The Church, however, must seek that awareness of mission, not through the lenses of Marx, but only by recourse to repentance and renewed proclamation of the Word of the Lord! A resolution to which LT is deliberately blind.

LT simply proposes to lead the Church down the road of violence and rebellion laid out by Marx.

Gutierrez puts it this way (in what, the reader must remember, is commonly touted as the "classic" statement of Liberation Theology): "Participation in the process of liberation is an obligatory and privileged *locus* for Christian life and reflection" (43:49). Far from submission to the Church, LT intends to impose its own "obligation" upon the Body of Christ: participate in "the process of liberation"—as defined by Marxism—or forego both "Christian life and reflection!" So the child confronts the Mother!

Gutierrez adds: "In Latin America, the Church must [!] place itself squarely within the process of revolution, amid the violence which is present in different ways" (43:138). Now that Marx has illumed the "way," the Body of Christ *must* obediently follow!

But Gutierrez is serious about it: "Rather than define the world in relation to the religious phenomenon, it would seem that religion should be redefined in relation to the profane" (43:67). While not the clearest of language, the import is unmistakable: let Marxism set the agenda for the Church, rather than the other way around!

And Gutierrez can live with the implication: "This presupposes an 'uncentering' of the Church, for the Church must cease considering itself as the exclusive place of salvation and orient itself towards a new and radical service of the people" (43:256)—a "service" defined, not by Christ's "teaching them to do all that I have commanded you," but defined by ideology!

Gutierrez' Church is not "uncentered," but re-centered, and gathers about the words of Marx instead of the Word of God!

Indeed, Gutierrez arrogantly lays claim to calling the Church herself into being; proclamation of his "gospel means convening a 'church' " (39:26)!

Marxism in the form of Liberation Theology will "convene" *the* Church, no less!!

José Comblin has it that there can be no "real people of God if Christians are not in the process of becoming an assembly of free persons struggling against the state and its powers. The church as an institution is Christian only [!] if it supports and defends such a people" (5:195).

The Church does not guide the Liberationist! Rather, the theologian lays down law to the Church! Law derived, not from the Word of God but from the word of Marx!

Evidence of LT's rebellion against the Church could be multiplied, but the conclusion will be the same:

LT's ninth sacrifice to Marxism: the Church!

10. Tenth Doctrinal Victim: Eschatology

The term "eschatology" is derived almost directly from the Greek (*eschaton*) and means doctrine of the "end-time" or "last things."

Various "theologies of hope" dabble in eschatology, framing theories as to what is around the corner, or might be if the theologian is obeyed.

Jürgen Moltmann puts it thus: "In the medium of hope our theological concepts become not judgments which nail reality down to what it is, but anticipations which show reality its prospects and its future possiblities" (69:35-36). Something of an ambitious program for a theologian, one might think, more commensurate with the deity: to "show reality its prospects and its future possiblities!" And what of those "prospects" when theologians differ, to say nothing of their forever altering the perception of what "possiblities" to dangle before history? Does it not threaten those who take them seriously with a certain dizziness?

Moltmann continues: "The theologian is not concerned merely to supply a different *interpretation* of the world, of history and of human nature, but to *transform* them in expectation of a divine transformation" (69:84). The theologian takes the lead, and God ratifies the "transformation!" But the transformation happens to take its lineaments from Marx!

It is said to have been Lenin's view that when a culture begins to think of its present in terms of eschatology, it betrays evidence of spiritual disintegration (52:103). No doubt Marxists welcome, therefore, the efforts of theologians like Moltmann and Wolfhart Pannenburg, in association with Marxists like Ernst Bloch, to impose such a focus upon the West.

We know by now what eschatological anticipations animate Liberation Theology: the expectation of a "new" society and a "new" human being via the process of rebellion, and we will not multiply quotations to make the point.

What is of concern here is that LT eschatology is Marxist rather than Christian, for several reasons:

1) Eschatology means, the reader will recall, doctrine of the "end-time."

If words mean what they denote, eschatology points to time's *end!* When the clock of history ticks its last moment, *what then?* That is the eschatological question.

The "end" in view here has a double significance: a) the "end" of time for each of us denoted by death, and b) the "end" of time for all mankind and its works together, denoted by what the Bible calls the Last Day.

There might be differences of interpretation as to *how* what happens after the "end" does in fact take place, but the Bible leaves no doubt as to *what* the "end" means for each and all of mankind:

"And as it is appointed unto men once to die, but after this the judgment . . ." (Heb. 9:27).

Again: "For we must all appear before the judgment seat of Christ, so that each may receive good or evil, according to what he has done in the body" (II Cor. 5:10).

Further: "For he will render to every man according to his works . . ." (Rom. 2:6).

And from the lips of Jesus Himself: "For the hour is coming when all who are in the tombs will hear his voice and come forth, those who have done good, to the resurrection of life, and those who have done evil to the resurrection of judgment" (John 5:28-29).

"But the day of the Lord will come like a thief," St. Peter writes to us, "and then the heavens will pass away with a loud noise, and the elements will be dissolved with fire, and the earth and the works that are upon it will be burned up" (II Pet. 3:10).

And thereafter follows the universal judgment so vividly pictured by the Christ in Matthew 25: "When the Son of man comes in his glory, and all the angels with him, then he will sit on his glorious throne. Before him will be gathered all the nations, and he will separate them one from another as a shepherd separates the sheep from the goats." The reader will notice that this separation is made before a word of judgment has been pronounced, meaning that each comes to this awesome post-temporal assize as already "sheep" or as already "goat." And of those who made themselves "goats" in the time alloted to them, the Judge says, "Depart from me, you cursed, into the eternal fire prepared for the devil and his angels," while to those who did His bidding He decrees, "Come, O blessed of my Father, inherit the kingdom prepared for you from the foundation of the world . . ." (Matt. 25:41; 34).

This is, in brief, biblical eschatology. It takes "end" in "end-time" seriously. Clearly to be distinguished from a Marxist/LT eschatological vision of the "sinned-against" settling accounts with "sinners" via violent rebellion.

2) Not only does LT temporalize eschatology to fit its Marxist commitment, but it is obliged to ignore the individuating character of biblical eschatology. Christian eschatology knows us one by one!

The ideological slogan of "class struggle" submerges the individual in the group. The bourgeoisie are hated as a class. The proletariat act as a class. As liberated from conscience by the ideological slogan of "class struggle," the individual proletarian can be persuaded to do violence against the individual bourgeois which would, apart from the class context, appall him. Responsiblity for behavior can be, and is (!), shifted from the individual to the class, from the act to the context.

But eschatology cuts through all this and sets the individual himself and herself before the celestial Judge, wholly and only responsible for the record which reads "sheep" or "goat."

Moral responsiblity becomes, in biblical eschatology, as unsharable as a toothache, as singular as every act of decision. *Each* will be judged, we are told, according to what *each* has done, be it good or evil—as defined by the Word, not justified by ideology.

Theologians of "hope" may set other "programs" for history, and Marxists like Trotsky may dream of temporal life cleansed of all evil and prolonged for centuries, but time itself will *end,* according to the Bible, and after that, every*one* comes to judgement alone and lifted quite out of the context, and excuses, of class struggle.

It is small wonder that LT willingly sacrifices a "sound and solid" doctrine of eschatology to its Marxist commitments. If the voice of biblical eschatology were heard in LT propaganda, all who are seduced into violence by the ideology might well ponder the eschatalogical consequences of their action in quite different terms than those laid down by theologies of hope.

3) The great *Divine Comedy* of Dante teaches what is sometimes called "realized" or "proleptic" eschatology—though those who use these baffling terms rarely have Dante in mind.

It is Dante's theme (echoed by C.S. Lewis in his book *The Great Divorce*) that time's end only certifies each one's passage to the eternal residence we have been preparing ourselves to occupy in every moment, every decision, every step of our temporal way. Thus, those who prefer hell to heaven demonstrate that preference by persistent rebellion to the will of God as revealed in the Scriptures, and at the "end" go accordingly to the place they have thus fitted themselves to inhabit forever. They could be 'comfortable' nowhere else! Those who seek God and strive after doing His Law find death the transition, Dante teaches, to residence in God's presence, perhaps, for Dante, after some purification in purgatory. C.S. Lewis pictures those who have deliberately chosen citizenship in Hades as quite unable to endure heaven, even given the chance to visit there.

Dante's intent is clear: to let the lengthening shadow, or growing radiance, of our eschatological destiny give us pause or genuine hope in the moral tensions of each moment. A doctrine of the "end-time" quite different from that mounted by ideologists!

In a word, LT's tenth doctrinal sacrifice to Marxism: a biblical eschatology!

11. Summary

Not only is Liberation Theology structured by the four fundamentals of Marxism, but—and no doubt because this is so—LT sacrifices to its Marxist commitment ten fundamentals of the Christian faith:

1. LT ignores the Fall.
2. Denies that death reflects the penalty upon the Fall.
3. Makes God the first Marxist.
4. Makes Jesus the author of subversion.
5. Rules out the Atonement.
6. Distorts conversion.
7. Perverts the meaning of Love.
8. Transforms Christian "works" into Marxist praxis.
9. Subjects the Church to Marxist mandates.
10. Forfeits a sound eschatology.

The list might be lengthened.

But it is enough to show what taking Marxist "help" in the analysis and cure of personal and social evils costs Christian theology.

Note: Liberation Theology and Marxism?

Liberation Theology really makes no secret of its commitment to Marxism.

This is evident from its appropriation of the four fundamentals of Marxism to structure its own approach to man and history.

LT is also deliberately ideological. This is obvious from its adoption of Marxist slogans—class struggle and liberation—and from its Marxist analysis of evil and its cure, and, finally, from the ideological subversion of the Bible and basic Christian doctrines to Marxist dictates.

1. Both Marxist and Christian?

Might LT, however, also be Christian?

Not at all! That is, not unless Marx himself was mistaken in making atheism fundamental to his system. Theism and atheism do not mix. Jesus said that long before Marx echoed it:

"No one can serve two masters; for either he will hate the one and love the other, or he will be devoted to the one and despise the other. You cannot serve God and mammon" (Matt. 6:24).

LT really makes no secret of its "rereading" the Bible and reformulating the basic doctrines we have discussed. And what is evident to the reader is that the Marxist master undoes the teaching of Bible and Church in each instance. LT's devotion is to its Marxism. In obedience to that devotion, LT shreds the Bible, distorts tradition and sets itself against and above the Church.

If Christianity be defined by the Bible and the creeds historically drawn from the Bible, as it certainly must be, then LT has no claim to inclusion in what these define as the Christian community.

We of course make no pretense of judging the Liberation Theologian's ultimate destiny, nor of hurling anathemas upon him. That is solely the Lord's affair, and the business of the Church.

We only say, on the basis of what has been presented above, to which much more of the same could be added:

Liberation Theology: Marxist!

An amalgam of Marxism-Christianity: Impossible!

Every effort to create such a hybrid plays only to the recurrent advantage of Marxism!

2. *Of Rhetoric and Justice*

The question might be raised: has only the "worst" of Liberation Theology been selected above to make what is in consequence but a distorted profile of LT?

No doubt we have chosen quotations apt to the point in hand, but they only accent rather than misrepresent the drift of LT "theological reflection." We have, in each section, tried to set commonly accepted Christian doctrine in contrast with LT's position on each matter. Unless it be possible to deny and affirm the same doctrine at the same time, what has been quoted above presents, to the best of our ability, an accurate delineation.

The question might, however, be framed differently: have expressions which would give LT a more favorable visage been deliberately omitted?

Does not José Comblin, for example, say, "The weakness of Marxism begins when it attempts to build a new society?" And, "in Marxist revolution there is no freedom for the people, only for the party" (5:219,220)?

Yes, so Comblin does say. But it is, as any reader of his whole volume knows, precisely the kind of "saying" that LT condemns in the Church, namely words without praxis. If the Liberation Theologian took seriously that cardinal deficiency of Marxism, he would—one might suppose—launch a vigorous effort to liberate LT from its Marxist orientation. For Marxism, he is saying, emerges as the absolute antithesis of what LT claims to be pursuing: freedom for the people!

Is Comblin's critique of Marxism here normative or rhetorical? Does he, then, review his treatise, and proceed to cleanse it of all Marxist ideology? Does he sound the alarm, and warn LT that the Marxist path leads to tyranny?

Comblin does no such thing!

"A revolution," he goes on to say, "is to be judged at first by the kind of society it intends to create" (5:221).

Note, "intends . . . !"

This immediately gets Marxism—and Comblin/LT—off the hook! The kind of society which Marx and Engels, Lenin and Trotsky, even Stalin and Khrushchev "intended" to create is the classless utopia which baits their ideology for the unwary. What invariably perverts Marxists' intentions into totalitarian reality is the innate depravity they themselves illustrate so vividly and ignore so blindly—a depravity to which LT is also oblivious.

With a nice indifference to logic, then, on one page Comblin has found Marxist societies infected with party tyranny, and on the next he judges Marxism by its intentions. Perhaps this is what LT would call "dialectical" thinking, and the old saw describes as having and eating your cake at the same time.

To quote the Liberation Theologian, then, on his occasional, perhaps rhetorical, disclaimers on Marxism or other elements in his "theological reflections," would itself be an inaccurate representation of the thrust of LT.

Like Marxism, LT constitutes a fairly consistent ideology. Between them there is a parallel so close as to constitute essentially an identity.

Let us try a final summary:

Marx finds the cause of human evil rooted, not in man himself, but in the class struggle resulting from capitalist relations of production. He advocates the cure of human evil through the violent overthrow of the system which sustains those relations of production. And he predicts the emergence of a "new" man in a liberated society after the debris of the revolution is swept away.

LT adopts the same scheme, and deceptively clothes it in theological language selectively adapted from the Bible. For LT, God sets man from the beginning in the context of class struggle; God demonstrates His preference for the victims in that struggle through the Exodus from Egypt. Evil is not rooted, therefore, in man's nature, but in the way he was ushered into history. Christ comes to illustrate the divine identification with the poor and oppressed. Himself a revolutionary, Jesus challenges the Church to participation in the violent struggle which will at last make man "new." Only Liberation Theology, forged in the midst of the Latin American situation, correctly perceives the biblical pattern implicit in man's call to self-redemption via rebellion.

Apparently Marx was, so far as LT is concerned, "the last of the Old Testament prophets"—and surely most reliable among them, after all.

But the question might still be phrased another way, already suggested in our Introduction: have we ignored the wide diversity among Liberation Theologians?

We have, to the contrary, found the Liberationists commonly referring to each other and themselves as "we," and sharing one core of content and perspective which makes reference to Liberation Theology as an entity possible.

But does not Hugo Assmann, for example, admit that so many Christologies are current in Latin America that, "there is no room for an exhaustive analysis of all the Christs being preached here" (39:139)?

Yes, Assmann does say that: "so many Christs . . . !"

Can someone who takes the Jesus of Nazareth as Lord and Savior say "so many Christs" without apology?

Many Christologies, indeed! But many "Christs?"

But these many LT Christs also share one core characteristic: no appeal is made to Bible, tradition or Church as authoritative voice for bringing order out of a shameful Christological chaos! In this LT is of one mind! Nor does this Theology appeal to creed or tradition or to the Bible as inspired Word of God to judge other LT deviations from orthodoxy. Instead LT is also of one voice in sitting in critical judgement upon Bible, Church and tradition.

Still more, LT is at one in canonizing individualism as against both Bible and Church. And LT is unanimous in acknowledging Marx as master.

Assmann is sure of that: "The basic reference points of traditional theology, the Bible and tradition (however the latter term may be understood), do not suffice for doing theology because they are not directly accessible . . . Praxis, then, becomes the basic reference point for any truly contextual theology" (5:135).

And "praxis," as we have observed, is central, not only to LT, but to Marxism.

PART **V**

Orthodoxy and Liberation

For Thine is the power. . . .

Matthew 6:13

The direction of the American Revolution remained committed to the foundation of freedom and the establishment of lasting institutions, and to those who acted in this direction nothing was permitted that would have been outside the range of civil law.

Hannah Arendt

For He spoke, and it came to be; He commanded, and it stood forth.

Psalm 33, verse 9

Christopher Dawson, in his work Religion and Culture, *sees in Christianity the first cause of the modern progress of science. . . . This is also the thought of Arnold Toynbee, Max Weber, and others.*

Piero Gheddo

Without the Bible we fall into nothing.

Karl Jaspers

12

Authentic Liberation

Liberation Theology defrauds the poor—and the rich!—of Latin America by seeking the living among the dead (Luke 24:5), that is seeking the Word of Truth in the words of Marx!

That this is the issue between orthodox Christianity and LT was made clear by Pope John Paul II in his brusque rejection of Liberationism at Puebla, Mexico, in January, 1979.

Speaking to a convocation of Latin American priests and bishops, some of them Liberationist, John Paul said:

"As pastors, you keenly realize that your chief duty is to be teachers of the truth: not a human, rational truth but of the truth that comes from God. That truth includes the principle of authentic human liberation, 'You will know the truth, and the truth will set you free' (John 8:32)."

The Pope's words were probably as rudely dismissed by some of his listeners as they were when first enunciated by Jesus, whose listeners sneered, "We . . . have never been in bondage to any one. How is it that you say, 'You will be made free'?" (John 8:33). Those enslaved by the Lie are the last to find that out.

John Paul goes on to say: "It is the one and only truth that offers a solid basis for an adequate 'praxis'. . . . From it will flow options, values, attitudes, and behavior patterns that can give direction and definition to our Christian living, that can create new human beings and then a new humanity through the conversion of the individual and social conscience" (30:59).

What Liberation Theology thinks to find in Marxism—freedom, adequate praxis and the "new man"—is on the contrary to be sought, the Pope says, in the "truth."

And this genuinely liberating "truth" is revealed to mankind through the Bible, not in the words of *Das Kapital!*

Liberation Theology inserts the wrong words into the Latin American situation. Truth, not ideology, liberates! Truth, not ideology, recreates! Truth, not ideology, takes constructive incarnation in progressive practice and socio-economic justice.

What the Pope refers to as "truth," we will, in what follows, commonly refer to as Christian "orthodoxy." It is from this perspective that we have mounted the critique of LT in the preceding sections.

By orthodoxy we understand enunciation of God's "truth" in "straight speech"—"straight" as measured by the canon (or rule) of the Scriptures (literally the Greek *ortho-doxa* implies the expression of "sound opinion," while *hetero*doxy means the expression of the opinion of one's own "choice," ungoverned by the canon.)

It is God's truth, John Paul is saying (at Puebla and since), as spoken in straight speech that has the power to clear the Latin American air of the theological haze generated by an amalgam of Marxism/LT.

The words of Marx and the Word of "truth" have both left tracks in history. We have already stressed Marx's track record, one of tyranny, brutality and slavery:

1) Wherever sown, the words of Marx spring up as the totalitarian state—a system so oppressive, so brutal, so un-liberating and anti-human that no Communist government dares submit itself to uncoerced referendum by the people.

2) Across nineteen centuries of history, despite aberration and setback, the Word of "truth," that is the Word of God preached, has had effects so radical, so decisive and so creative as to make the words of Marxism/LT parochial and narrowly materialistic by contrast.

Very briefly, the Word of God, absorbing the Greco-Roman heritage, flowered into Western civilization. That is its record.

Since the Reformation, moreover, that Word has evoked the political democracy which has freed every phase of Western culture for gigantic, progressive strides. So much so that Dutch historian Arend Theodoor van Leeuwen can argue persuasively in his *Christianity In World History* (88) that the non-Western world eagerly reaches out to grasp the fruits of Western technocracy and political liberty, even in the face of its own ideologists who denounce Western "imperialism" and scorn programs of "development." So eagerly indeed does the "Third World" yearn for Western culture, that while Marxism/LT pour vituperation upon the West in propaganda, they in fact try to seduce the Latin American poor with anticipation of a share in Western-like abundance and freedom!

What the Word of Truth had the power to do in the West, that Word can do for Latin America and the rest of the "Third World"—all the more rapidly if the process were not corrupted by ideology, whose track record always leads in but one direction—into the pit of totalitarianism!

In the sections which follow we will briefly sketch some of the propulsion given by orthodox "straight speech" to Western progress.

One conclusion will be, we think, inevitable: hope for liberty, justice and socio-economic progress in Latin America rests in the spreading dawn of the light of "truth" as proclaimed by the "straight speech" of the Church, and not in lengthening the shadows of ideological terrorism.

At issue is this: *whose* word?

Words guide praxis and weave the web of history.

The Word of God liberates!

The words of Marx enslave!

13

Root of Freedom

A free people all too casually takes freedom for granted. We hardly take note that political liberty spreads its mantle of protection over even those who wish to undermine it.

Taking that relative rarity, democracy, as much for granted as we take the presence of sun and moon, stars and sea, winter and summer, we rarely pause to wonder how the West won a freedom which has created a culture that, as van Leeuwen says, the rest of the world eagerly yearns to acquire.

Why the West and not elsewhere? Why do technology, medicine, industrial know-how with all its fruits, and the like, all radiate out from the West? Why do even the enemies of the West themselves enjoy the fruits of a culture they at least pretend to condemn?

Surely the Western world did not just happen?

Why, then?

The answer is that Christianity, long before Horace Greeley's celebrated advice, "went West!"

In the mystery of divine Providence, St. Paul was sent to what became the Western world—largely so defined by the fact that Christianity took root and blossomed there.

The West flowers upon roots deep laid by Christian orthodoxy. And Western political liberty stems from a Christianity focused by the Reformation upon the sound *preaching* of the Word of Truth—an emphasis upon the pulpit implied in Pope John Paul's indictment of LT, but one which has yet to take profound hold upon the Catholic Church in Latin America.

We are well aware that the West has its defects, some of them glaring, and grows its crop of in-house critics—who unintentionally testify that freedom is hospitable. Bear it in mind: democracy always makes room, in ways ideologists cannot understand, for its most vocal enemies, who ab-use the liberties which define the West to accent its discontents and undermine its foundations. Jacques Ellul takes account of some of them in his *Betrayal Of The West*—analyzing treason of the same kind that robbed France of the will to withstand Nazi militarism even before World War II began.

But democracy's most virulent critics cannot avoid bearing witness to the worth of the system they try to denigrate. Their own abuse of freedom confirms democracy's dedication to it! Compare the liberating atmosphere created by Western political institutions to the paralyzing miasma of fear that cripples the tongue and blights association even among the most loyal devotees of Communist autocracy.

As pointed out earlier, the question, "Why . . ?" cannot be raised in Marxist states, while democratic states deliberately protect the questioner's right to pose and respond to it.

How absolute are the distinctions between Western democracy and Marxist totalitarianism: democracy builds in, as totalitarianism walls out, a political mechanism for self-correction! Democracy welcomes, as totalitarianism avoids, periodic recourse to the judgment of the people. In a word, democracy recognizes all men's disposition to faults and is as open as totalitarianism is closed to self-correction.

We have traced Communism to its origins in the words of Karl Marx.

We are contending here that Western democracy owes its origins to the Word of God.

To trace fruit to root, let us take account of some important distinctions.

14

Energy and Power

Orthodoxy turns for transforming *power* to the Word of God.

Liberation Theology hopes to find transforming *energy* focused by the words of Marx.

While we often use the terms "energy" and "power" interchangeably, for an understanding of historical effects of ideology and orthodoxy, the difference between them is crucial.

Let us begin by asking: what is "energy?"

Energy is integral to nature. The cosmos seems to consist of vibrant energy made mysteriously accessible as objects to our senses—this is the testimony of modern physics. Science does not explain energy; it simply uses it.

Everywhere and all the time energy in countless forms sings the song of the Creator to those who can hear.

From "the beginning," God endowed the universe with energy: "And God said, 'Let there be light;' and there was light" (Gen. 1:3). Light is the typical form of energy. And the awesome depths of energy invested by God in His creation have most lately surfaced in the shattering of the atom.

God put energy under man's control. You are, God said to Adam, to "subdue the earth" (Gen. 1:28). Man has woven his civilizations upon the loom of time through the subjugation of natural energies to control through his science.

But energy is finite. There are things energy cannot do. These limitations begin to appear when we consider how the success of applied science tempts theorists to devise "scientific" formulas for focusing energy upon the solution of specifically human problems. Scientists assume that what energy can do in physics it can be trained to do in psychology. Theorists suppose that what propels men to the moon should mend fractures in the soul.

Marx formulates his "scientific" ideology, for example, to focus the energy of rebellion upon the elimination of evil. Marx planned it that way: "Material force must be overthrown by material force. But theory also becomes a material force once it has gripped the masses" (55:257).

Behaviorists like B.F. Skinner want to impose scientific formulas upon human behavior to focus energy upon solving social dilemmas. Freudian and other forms of psychiatry entice the patient to muster his own energies for lifting himself out of frustration or despair by his own introspective and retrospective bootstraps. Cults and sects look to the energies of the occult, while others rest hopes on the energies presumably available to positive thinking, or to the optimistic outlook and accessible to the sheer will to "succeed."

Always the hope is to find in energy a key to resolving social problems by changing human nature.

But energy is, we have just noted, bounded by time and space. Energy has its limitations. As applied within the range of its competence, energy works miracles. The Western world is built upon the control of energy.

But energy falls short of resolving precisely the grave human defects that sow tares among the wheat of progress and today threaten the earth with atomic incineration.

Even the energies of human passion fall short of human reformation, though ideologists call upon them. Marxist Che Guevara said it plainly (the italics are his): "*Hatred is an important factor in the struggle,* an implacable hatred of the enemy, a hatred that spurs man to overcome his natural limitations and makes him an effective machine for killing, a machine both vigorous and cold" (38:128). Lenin, Khrushchev and various Soviet theoreticians can be quoted to the same effect, as can China's Mao Tse Tung.

Marxism has indeed become a devastating socio-political weapon by engaging hatred in the deployment of human energies for the purpose of violent rebellion. But "an effective machine for killing" lacks the strength to bring a new world to birth. And, as we have been observing, far from transforming the "old" man into the "new," the energies put to the service of violence by ideological hatred have killed so many as to drench the earth with human blood—and bind the survivors with shackles of steel!

Indeed, every quest for a philosophy, or science, or potion or draught of some mystical energy to cure the soul of propensity to evil and the body of drift into decay has gleamed like a star on vanishing horizons, and faded away in the harsh light of reality.

No manipulation of energy, physical or psychic or dialectical, ever recalls man from death, nor stays life's curtain from falling.

In brief, energy produces the "novel"—rearranging the pieces—every day; but making man "new" waits upon another requisite not found among human resources!

That requisite is *power!*

Power alone creates.

Power alone recreates.

Power belongs to God.

Power called the "new" out of nothing "in the beginning," and power recalls fallen man back to the "new" wherever the Word of God—the vehicle of power—is preached and believed.

Power is God's alone: "For thine is the power," concludes every lip that utters the Lord's Prayer (Matt. 6:13).

"All power is given me in heaven and in earth," says the risen Lord to His disciples just before His ascension (Matt. 28:18).

Power is a divine attribute, never shared with man. We can be its beneficiaries, but never its masters. God places power at our service, via His Word, but never at our behest.

We control energy; power comes to regain control of us.

The words of Marx dispose energy.

The Word of God conveys power.

The open secret of Western progress does not reside in energy alone.

The West has flourished upon power ushered into its history via God's Word, a power which changed man and society, and set the uses of energy to widespread public good.

The oppressed who look to the energies of hatred fixed upon rebellion for their liberation inevitably find themselves the victims of ideologues who beguile them with false hopes and transient fantasies. Energy has not made the ideologue "new," and will not free his victims from bondage.

On balance of track records:

Ideology has ridden the coattails of energy focused upon *rebellion* to the autocratic state, where all but the dictators are reduced to proletarians!

The Word of orthodoxy has, on the other hand, funneled divine power into the West for fueling the most progressive *revolutions* the world has ever known, where freedom beckons to all.

Let us turn, then, to another distinction.

15

Rebellion or Revolution

The distinction we have observed between *energy* and *power* is reflected in history by social upheavals often confused. If we are to think clearly about the practical difference between the words of Marx and the Word of God we must emphasize an easily ignored distinction between two key terms in contemporary discussion, the terms *revolution* and *rebellion.*

Rebellion develops out of the deployment of energy through ideology.

Revolution emerges from the deployment of energy under the governance of power, that is of God's Word.

Though commonly used interchangeably—occasionally also in this book—the terms revolution and rebellion are not, in fact, synonyms for the same kind of social cataclysm.

Both do, it is true, denote overthrow of the status quo.

Both denote political transformation.

Both may connote violent transition.

But rebellion differs from revolution as dream differs from design, as twilight contrasts with day, as the word of Marx differs from the Word of God.

Rebellion exploits energy to rend and destroy. Rebellion majors in negation. The rebel energetically demolishes a socio-political system in passionate worship of ideology. But rebellion typically leaves weaving the pattern of whatever comes after destruction to the warp of rebel leadership and the woof of circumstance. Rebellion shatters, but what rises from the ashes is absolute authority in some shrewd leader's hands.

Revolution, on the other hand, draws upon power to transform. Revolution effects a transition to an end clearly envisioned before revolt is undertaken. The revolutionary substitutes a clearly perceived and formulated socio-political system for the one overthrown.

The rebel aims to destroy, hoping for the best; the revolutionary aims to replace the worse with the better, knowing the "new" system he wants.

Christian orthodoxy has authored revolution; Marxism authors rebellion; LT apes Marxism.

And of crucial importance: while the rebel leadership seizes political authority as its due, the revolutionary leadership has, historically, done battle to transfer political power into the hands of the people. Of this the American Revolution is typical.

In her study titled *On Revolution,* editor and author Hannah Arendt quotes Saint-Just, one of the leaders of the French Revolution of 1789, as declaring, "All must be permitted to those who act in the revolutionary direction."

"It would be difficult to find," Ms Arendt writes, "in the whole body of revolutionary oratory, a sentence that pointed with greater precision to the issues about which the founders and the liberators, the men of the American Revolution and the men in France, parted company. The direction of the American Revolution remained committed to the foundation of freedom and the establishment of lasting institutions, and to those who acted in this direction nothing was permitted that would have been outside the range of civil law. . . . The lawlessness of the 'all is permitted' sprang here from the sentiments of a heart whose very boundlessness helped in the unleashing of a stream of boundless violence" (3:87).

Ms Arendt emphasizes the distinction we are drawing. She finds the spirit of rebellion characteristic of the French Revolution of 1789, and the spirit of revolution characteristic of the American Revolution of 1776.

In a rebellion "all must be permitted!"

In a revolution "nothing was permitted that would have been outside the range of civil law" to which the revolutionaries had committed themselves.

It is, obviously, of enormous importance to Latin America whether efforts to resolve its massive socio-economic problems are made via rebellion (a la Marx/LT) or revolution (empowered by the Word of God freely preached).

Ms Arendt traces the rebel spirit of 1789 to the intrusion of emotional sympathy for the impoverished people of France, and she concludes that the endless violence and bloodshed of that French Revolution were owing to the unlimited nature of sentimentality. She traces the orderly transition characteristic of 1776 to the self-disciplined character of those who guided the American Revolution.

But both the spirit of 1776 in New England and the spirit of 1789 in Paris had roots.

The spirit of 1776 grew out of the Word of God preached by generations of orthodox colonial pulpits.

The men of France, 1789, mounted a *rebellion* upon foundations laid by the ideology of Rousseau, just as Lenin and Trotsky forged *rebellion* in Russia in 1917 upon ideological foundations laid by Karl Marx.

All depends upon whose "word" is the motivating force.

In both the France of 1789 and Russia of 1917, the ideological focus was on demolition, in Hegelian terms upon negation. What might come next was played, so to speak, by ear. And the world knows what did come next: after bloody interludes, rebellion fell into the dictatorship of Napoleon in France and into the monstrous tyranny of Stalin in Russia.

While in America what came after 1776 forged itself into the "last best hope of mankind!"

Words matter, and never more than when they are either the Word of God or the words of the ideologue.

Only when that distinction is taken seriously can a progressive transformation of man and his world be anticipated.

16

Why Rebellion Becomes Totalitarian

The direction which history takes depends upon which "word" sets the pace for human events. To which drummer, in the metaphor of Thoreau, will mankind march?

The word of man, fashioned into ideology and echoing the Lie of the Devil, evokes rebellion!

The Word of God, preached and taught through the Church has, in the past four centuries, mounted democratic revolutions!

Rebellion fades into tyranny; revolution flowers into democracy.

And why does rebellion fail to achieve the goals used to promote it?

Quite obviously because of some inherent difference between the words of man and the Word of God. Man's word is finite; God's Word infinite.

Like the energy which it disposes, no ideology embodies limitless possibility. No human idea is infinitely fertile.

It becomes clear, then, that the inherent limitations of rebellion are implicit in the finite resources of the ideas that generate it.

The ideology mounts a rebellion. It succeeds, and history rushes to meet it. But the words of ideology, however sophisticated, quickly encounter circumstances they are unfitted to master. The rebellion which ideology so effectively stimulates soon exhibits the limitations of the ideologue. Marx's "dictatorship of the proletariat" cannot find in Marxism the resilience required to cope with challenges requiring constructive resolution.

Unlike the Word of God, the word of Marx, genius that he was, comes bound by Marx's horizons; how could any man's ideology, however dialectical, cope with the unceasing vicissitudes of history? The living present slips through the crevices of the static ideology. Naturally so!

So the great Russian novelist Leo Tolstoy foresaw: "Even if that which Marx predicted should happen," Tolstoy recorded in his journal in August, 1898, "then the only thing that will happen is that despotism will be passed on. Now the capitalists rule, but then the directors of the working people will rule" (81:259). Tolstoy echoes the warning which the other great Russian novelist of the time, Fyodor Dostoevsky, wrote his prophetic novel *The Possessed,* also translated as *The Devils* (26), to voice. Warnings which the ideologues, with customary arrogance, brushed aside; warnings which no doubt echo eerily down the corridors of the Gulag Archipelago.

If the ideology triumphs, as it has in the Communist states, its internal limitations begin to surface. And when the ideology nears exhaustion, the rebel leadership carries on through brute force, arbitrary administration and thinly camouflaged egotism. This is why rebellion always goes totalitarian, exploding the ideology's illusions at the expense of the populace it pretends to "liberate."

Every Communist state betrays the same symptoms. The embalmed words of Marx, Engels and Lenin fall far short of mastering the unpredictabilities of history. As the ideology wanes the tyranny waxes. A wearied Marxism lingers on in slogans mouthed by rote, and reechoes in ceremonial speeches made without conviction and heard without enthusiasm. The ideology spreads but a threadbare cloak over what Harvard Professor Adam Ulam aptly characterizes in his book *The Bolsheviks* as "cynicism masquerading as dialectic in defense of one-party rule" (87:453).

There is another Word. Not of man, but of God!

And in unmistakable contrast to ideology, Christian orthodoxy commits social transformation to that omnicompotent Word. For it is God alone who knows "the end from the beginning" (Is. 46:10). In His Word resides the power, the inexhaustible resource, the infinite flexibility and endless fecundity which have lifted Western peoples to hitherto unscaled heights of progress.

And this is why, so long as that Word resounds across the land, democracies do not slip into totalitarianism! They cannot!

And this too is why the West depends far more than is popularly realized upon a continued proclamation of that Word from faithful pulpits!

Lacking the power of this Word, and committed to the energies manipulated by ideology, a society ruled by ideologues falls prey to cruel and arbitrary regimentation. Even the majestic vision of Marx, whose favorite phrase was the ancient aphorism, "Nothing human is alien to me," and who wrote with the riches of Western literature alive in his fingertips, has been dwarfed by the Communist state into the suffocating mediocrity so vividly portrayed by ex-Marxist Arthur Koestler in his *Darkness At Noon* (49)!

Nor will the delusion that one might have Marx without Communism avoid the inevitable declension: because the words of man are of finite capability, out of the travail of rebellion is inevitably born the totalitarian monster!

What real hope, then, is there for the Latin American poor in the ideological mouthings of Liberation Theology?

Yet, faithful to its penchant for Marxism, LT blindly opts for rebellion!

Hear Gutierrez: "It has been all the great social revolutions—the French and Russian, for example, to mention only two important milestones—together with the whole process of revolutionary ferment that they initiated which wrested—or at least began to—political decisions from the hands of an elite who were 'destined' to rule. Up to that time the great majority of people did not participate in political decisions or did so only sporadically and formally" (43:47).

But when did either of the Revolutions which Gutierrez takes as models ever in fact endow, or to the slightest degree "at least begin" to endow, participation in political decision-making upon "the great majority of people?" When did the French Directorate, or Lenin and Trotsky or Stalin or the current Soviet dictator ever betray the least intention of so doing? Where does a political "elite" rule with more obscene privilege and absolute authority than in Communist states?

Can it be that Liberationists never read—they surely do not heed—the warnings issued by one-time ideologists who helped bring Marxism into reality, saw their awesome mistake and somehow told the tale?

We are thinking, for example, of Jugoslav Communist Milovan Djilas, early a close associate of Joseph Tito, whose book describing the Marxist elite as *The New Class* put him behind bars.

"During my adult life," Djilas writes, "I have traveled the entire road open to a Communist: from the lowest to the highest rung of the hierarchical ladder, from local and national to international forums, and from the formation of the true Communist Party and organization of the revolution to the establishment of the so-called socialist society. No one compelled me to embrace or to reject Communism. I made my own decision according to my convictions, freely, in so far as a man can be free. . . . I cut myself off gradually and consciously, building up the picture and conclusions I present in this book" (24:vi).

And what is the "New Class" to which Djilas refers?

"This new class," he answers, "the bureaucracy, or more accurately the political bureaucracy, has all the characteristics of earlier ones as well as some new characteristics of its own"—all the faults of the Czar (Djilas is writing about the Soviet Union) plus additional enormities of its own. "Behind Lenin, who has all the passion and thought, stands the dull, gray figure of Joseph Stalin, the symbol of the difficult, cruel, and unscrupulous ascent of the new class to its final power. . . . The epoch of the practical men has set in. The new class has been created. It is at the height of its power and wealth, but it is without new ideas. . . . Smothering everything except what suited its ego, it has condemned itself to failure and shameful ruin" (24:38, 52, 69). And, we can add, condemned a whole nation to intolerable bondage!

Deaf as they are to a Djilas, totally insensitive as they seem to be to other anguished accounts of disillusionment with the Soviet experiment like, say, Victor Serge's *Memoirs Of A Revolutionary* (79), and apparently oblivious to how Marxism in Poland degrades human beings and the Church, what kind of creative leadership could a Gutierrez and his like provide toward the true liberation of an oppressed people?

As LT discredits itself, let the exploited turn to the "truth" in hope.

For that "truth" does liberate, and has lit the world of the West with the glow of freedom and political democracy.

17

A Deceptive Simplicity

There is a deceptive and baffling simplicity about the "truth" as proclaimed by orthodoxy.

That simplicity, oddly enough, complicates expression, now, of precisely what we believe to be the crux of this study.

St. Paul put the problem this way: "For Jews demand signs and Greeks seek wisdom, but we preach Christ crucified, a stumbling block to Jews and folly to Gentiles . . ." (I Cor. 1:22-23).

Transliterated into the context of ideology and revolution, Marxists demand rebellion and Liberationists echo them, while orthodoxy puts its trust in the Word of God vibrantly preached from courageous pulpits.

In a word, activists impatiently demand more immediate and palpable results than reliance upon a Word *preached* seems likely to produce. There seems to be something tame, if not frustrating, about waiting for social action upon a Word spoken without apparent immediate effect, week after week, pulpit after pulpit.

Only by looking around might the impatient activist be warned that the words of the ideologue which promise quick liberation do in fact deliver but more brutal tyranny.

And only by looking back does the impatient activist discover, no doubt to his surprise, that power has entered history, and creatively transformed it too, via that Word flowing so apparently innocuously from human lips.

Delivered from ideological blinders, the would-be rebel notices that nations which have enjoyed the proclamation of biblical "straight speech" have pushed progress far toward the dimensions he dreams of for impoverished peoples!

But to make this discovery implies the willing subordination of self, of ideology, of praxis, and of energies to the power of God's Word—requires in short *repentance* as we pointed out above! And, alas, by definition "rebels" would rather mount yet another desperate negation of their world than bow to the yoke of the Word.

At issue, as Hannah Arendt suggests without enunciating it, in the modern world (and in all worlds, ancient and future) is not "class" struggle but "word" struggle—*whose* words find willing believers and thus shape the course of history? To whose word will each of us turn? Whose word will each of us hear and heed? Whose word will shape the relation of rich to poor, of poor to rich, and of rich and poor to themselves? Whose word will focus energy upon constructive goals? Whose word will admit the power of God into human history? Whose word will peddle the Lie?

Whose word? or Word?

An activism which has learned the meaning of repentance, perhaps by pondering the awesome inhumanity of the ideological state, must learn to accustom itself to the fact that, unlike ideology, orthodoxy can come with no social blueprints, writes no scenarios for social overhaul, and never pretends to know in advance what the Word, faithfully proclaimed, will "do." Such a pretense would be ideological.

Orthodoxy is, from a secular and conspiratorial point of view, 'stuck' with a Word. This remains a grave defect to the militant rebel until, if ever, he realizes that his commitment, too, is to the word—of ideology!

It may be that only when it is perceived that this *Word* is the dynamic Speech of the living *God* that orthodoxy begins to, as 'tis said, make sense. But then orthodoxy's single-minded passion to get God's Word "out" is recognized as challenge enough to absorb all the energies that the most rebellious of would-be rebels could bring to it.

Persuading pulpits given to discoursing pop psych and parading current liturgical fashions to *preach the Word* is more than challenge enough, once the vision of what that Word can do has taken hold.

Recalling that Jesus Himself attributed His coming death simply to bearing witness to the Truth (not of Marx but of God) is challenge enough for all who dare to do the same. "But now you seek to kill me," Jesus says to those who accuse Him, "a man who has told you the truth which I heard from God . . ." (John 8:40). And to His disciples: "If the world hates you, know that it has hated me before it hated you. . . . If I had not come and spoken to them, they would not have sin; but now they have no excuse for their sin" (John 15:18, 22). To Pontius Pilate the Lord says: "For this I was born, and for this I have come into the world, to bear witness to the truth. Everyone who is of the truth hears my voice" (John 18:37).

Jesus comes to preach Truth. For that He sustains the Church.

It is divine Truth that sears the conscience, and not an ideology that soothes it, that transforms "old" into "new" men. The Church has a transforming Word to speak to rich and poor, to oppressor and oppressed that can accomplish revolution. It is *this* Word that the Lord Himself preached to the poor (Matt. 11:5)!

Does not one sense, reading between the lines of what they have written, that Marx, with Lenin and Trotsky after him, became at last bitterly aware that "wreckers" and "hooligans" were already perverting their visions and achievements, and had some fearful sense of the abyss yawning before a society of those who follow the wrong word? The fruit of the rebel tree, now as in Eden, betrays its seductive appearance with bitter taste.

Christ was not the model social rebel. He was the model preacher!

Behind the apparently impotent simplicity of the orthodox formula the Word preached to effect revolutionary change is modeled on Jesus the Christ, who was done to death for preaching the same Word! That is the risk, and the burden, He now as ever imposes upon His Church—and how few there be who rise to it! Let would-be rebels call the Church to its duty, and Marx can be forgotten!

The world does not lack for would-be rebels, especially for those who can combine rebellion with the security of the classroom or study. The world does not lack for speculators in the marketplace of ideas, especially those whose living is provided by a society committed to "education."

But the world sorely lacks and desperately needs pulpiteers who will risk, like their Lord, the hatred of those to whom they preach Truth. And the world desperately needs believers who will demand such preaching, and will support it with their bodies, if need be, when it is heard.

There have been such believers, who were inspired to democratic revolution—the kind Hannah Arendt speaks of—by such preaching. We will look at these brave models, hoping to inspire their like again.

18

The Word of Truth and Power

There is great mystery about words.

Linguists search in vain for the origins of human language.

The Greek philosopher Plato was so amazed that children could learn to use and understand words that he presumed some pre-existent state for mankind.

Without knowing precisely what words *are* or whence they come, we can know something of what words *do,* both in our use and in history.

God chose language to communicate power—in the beginning!

We use words to establish communion—or discord—among and within ourselves.

The "word" is the fulcrum of history, both personal and universal.

The book of Genesis opens with a litany to the power of speech. God summons being out of non-being—by a Word!

The Genesis creation account, which Marx rejects and LT (despite all its talk of the Creator) essentially ignores, is a symphony of oral evocation of being. Syllable by syllable across the inspired chapter God *speaks* (mind you, that is all!—and enough!) and behold, no-thing becomes some-thing!

Had not a speculative theology essentially robbed both Church and world of the impact of Genesis, how astounding we might perceive words, mere words, to be! God *spoke* and the cosmos appeared.

The inspired Psalmist summarizes: "For he spoke, and it came to be; he commanded, and it stood forth" (Ps. 33:9).

When even a hint of what this means occupies our consciousness, we instinctively are drawn to this elixir, this potion, this power—the great mystery of words!

And we come to perceive something of the miracle that can be wrought upon the human soul and human relations by the omnicompetent *Word* of God, using our language as His vehicle.

Far off? Unattainable? For only the initiate?

Not at all!

So close is God's Word to us, Moses says, that we need not look to heaven nor across the sea, "that we may hear it and do it. But the word is very near you; it is in your mouth and in your heart, so that you can do it" (Deut. 30:12-14). That is to say, God's Word comes in our own language, the speech upon our tongues interpreted within the self.

Christ sums up the thrust of the Scriptures in the response which Adam and Eve should have given (and we are obliged to give) to the same Tempter who faced Him: "It is written, 'Man shall not live by bread alone, but by every word that proceeds from the mouth of God' " (Matt. 4:4, quoting Deut. 8:3).

Notice that what the Devil suggested was exactly what ideology dangles before the poor: "If you are the Son of God," Satan says, "command these stones to become loaves of bread" (Matt. 4:3). No more apt summation of Marxist ideology could be made! In the three temptations of Jesus, Dostoevsky says in his "Legend Of The Grand Inquisitor," are etched out the basic options of human destiny: the hunger for goods, the lust for power and the passion of pride.

The Lord proclaims the Word of God as key to liberation.

So, in obedience to the Lord, does orthodoxy!

But not as a Word once spoken. Rather, as a Word forever active in the cosmos and awaiting faithful proclamation in all ages and places.

What God has called into being, His Word ever sustains: "Lift up your eyes on high and see: who created these? He who brings out their host by number, calling them all by name; by the greatness of his might, and because he is strong in power, not one is missing," declares the prophet (Is. 40:26). The Word communicates a divine power that extends from calling the stars to hold their courses to governing the fate of the sparrow and a hair from the head (Matt. 10:29-31).

Power-ful as was the Word "in the beginning" so powerful is that Word forever: "Heaven and earth," the Lord says, "will pass away, but my words will not pass away" (Matt. 24:35). Always powerful, and always there!

The reader has no doubt noticed that the term "Word" is subject to a certain deliberate ambiguity in the Scriptures. It always specifies the vehicle God employs for the transmission of His power, but it does so in various, related forms: 1) the term "Word" can denote the second Person of the Holy Trinity through whom God created and recreates; 2) the "Word" can denote Jesus of Nazareth, the second Person of the Holy Trinity incarnate in human flesh from the virgin Mary; 3) the "Word" can denote the vehicle provided by human language and recorded in the Scriptures; and 4) "Word" can mean the message of the

Bible proclaimed upon the human tongue in orthodox pulpits. Which of these inter-related foci is in view can be determined from the context.

Of absolutely crucial importance to the tensions between the words of ideology and the Word of God is the fact that divine power is transmitted into history via language—the "straight speech" of orthodoxy.

As observed above, linguistic science has been frustrated in its every effort to account for human speech by tracing language to its origins. This is because the human capacity for speech inheres in the Image of God in which man was created, and creation is inaccessible to science.

God made man a word-user. The function of language, in the beginning, was to provide means of communication between God and man—and man with man.

After the Fall, man was left a word-user to keep open the option of hearing again what God has to say and thus receiving the power which God alone has to give. Language thus becomes the potentially saving differentia of man's uniqueness among all created things.

God Himself proclaims the unmistakable centrality of the Word to human re-"new"-al when, subsequent to the Fall, and on its account, He commits His Son to incarnation in human flesh. God calls this incarnation of redemptive power *the Word:* "In the beginning was the Word, and the Word was with God, and the Word was God. . . . And the Word became flesh and dwelt among us, full of grace and truth" (John 1:1, 14).

In the power and under the guidance of God's Word—incarnate in the flesh of Jesus and audible upon the lips of His faithful ministry—the West has oustripped all the civilizations of the world!

In the guidance of God's Word!

The orthodox alternative to Liberation Theology is by no means a docile sanctification of the status quo. Orthodoxy is restless because the Truth is restless with anything short of perfection: "You, therefore, must be perfect, as your heavenly Father is perfect" (Matt. 5:48). But for the power to change things, orthodoxy turns to the Word of God rather than to the words of Marx!

This, we grant once more, seems pale stuff compared with the heady propaganda of violence. Seems so, that is, until the reader pauses long enough to be grasped by the fact that the "Word" we speak of is that of the living God!

It is, however unexciting mere preaching may seem to be, the Word of God as revealed in the Bible which has opened the West to its world-envied progress.

Let us examine that a little.

19

The Bible and the West

The power and guidance of God's Word enter human history via the Bible. Orthodoxy therefore calls the Bible, quite simply, the Word of God!

The distinguished contemporary philosopher, Karl Jaspers, says it plainly:

"Every time the question is asked whether Europe could exist or could possibly be without the Bible, but solely on its pre-biblical and Greek origins, the answer must always be that whatever we are, we are as the result of this biblical religion and the secularization that results from this religion, from the finest humanism to the motivations of modern science and the leaders of the great philosophies. In fact, without the Bible we fall into nothing" (38:36-37).

Orthodoxy says no more, and no less: "Without the Bible we fall into nothing!"

Were this but the message of LT to Latin America, the Pope need not have voiced his stern reprimand at Puebla, nor need the Vatican be focusing critical attention upon Liberation Theology.

But, taking its cue from Marx, LT says nothing of the kind!

Note that Jaspers speaks of "the secularization that results from this religion." He does not mean some secular perversion of Christianity. He means, rather, that God deliberately distinguished His creation from Himself. God made nature "secular" when, as we have already observed, He authorized man in the person of Adam to "subdue" the earth (Gen. 1:28).

God thus "secularized" His world to man's advantage. And wherever this message has gotten out, science has indeed subdued the world to the service of human progress.

Religions which, unlike Christianity, identify nature with the gods, and thus revere the world as sacred, hamper or preclude the development of experimental science and the appropriation of natural resources to human use.

"For a man of the third world," writes Father Piero Gheddo in his book, *Why Is The Third World Poor?*, "(and naturally I am not thinking of one who has received a modern education in the West) nature is to be contemplated, feared, submitted to, respected" (38:44).

Therefore, as Gheddo goes on to say, "Having no idea of man's dignity or any concept of progress, the relation between man and nature becomes one of contemplation, not of tension, discovery, and conquest on man's part. In the same way, work is looked upon purely as a means of subsistence, not an instrument for the improvement of one's own condition, and of the whole of society" (38:52).

The "Third World" is poor because, as we have pointed out, Christianity took, or was given, no root there. The Western world is blessed with myriad abundance because it learned from Christian orthodoxy that God does not identify Himself with what He has made. God, orthodoxy teaches, gives over the earth to man. Indeed, man is required from the beginning to honor God by developing for his own use all the potential resident in God's world.

That man's freedom to use the creation is marred by excessive waste and pollution no one denies. 'Tis the reflection of innate depravity. But that Western science and initiative have also put energy massively to human service, thanks to Christian orthodoxy, is denied only by the ideological fanatic.

Moreover, as German sociologist Max Weber was to point out, Christian orthodoxy recognized human labor as a basic form in which God is worshipped. And as Marx was to stress in his own context, it is human labor which underlies Western progress. *Labore est ora* (to work is to pray) speaks for more than the Benedictines in Western history; it is the accent of Christianity waiting to enrich impoverished peoples who can escape the constriction which ideology imposes upon free enterprise!

For it has been, and is, through *this* orthodox conception of his relation to the cosmos that Western man has "subdued" nature to achieve a degree and diffusion of economic "liberation" which Marxism and LT only caricature.

In this sense, Jaspers means, Christianity "secularizes" creation and opens its energies to human use. Harvey Cox stresses the same point in his popular *The Secular City*.

The Word of God has "liberated" the West to become what it is! And, as the late Union Seminary Professor Rheinhold Niebuhr was fond of pointing out, what Marxist ideologues really want, when obliged to define their goals, is the economic abundance and political self-determination which Christianity has brought to the West. Were the ideologist to admit this, however, he would lose the vehicle he intends to ride into political tyranny!

God's liberating Word is the Word of "truth" the Pope admonishes the Church to preach into the tensions of Latin America—and the world!

It is this infinitely fecund and powerful Word which holds out the only real hope that Latin America has of becoming what those who really care about "liberation" want it to be!

In summary:

Power is God's alone. He chooses to make transforming power, both personal and social, available to man via the Bible.

This is the motivating conviction of orthodoxy.

What, then, has been lacking in the under-developed society?

What, until recently, has not been proclaimed forthrightly to Latin American ears, those of poor and rich alike?

Quite simply: the Bible! The living Word of the living God! The Bible which Marxism scorns, LT shreds, and orthodoxy reveres!

What, then, is the source of true hope for Latin America?

The Bible, preached to pour its power into the depths of human need!

"Christopher Dawson, in his work *Religion and Culture*," Gheddo says, "sees in Christianity the first cause of the modern progress of science, because it is Christianity that freed man from the enslavement to nature, gave him knowledge of his dignity, and messianic hope to fight for—that is, a goal to approach in history and beyond. This is also the thought of Arnold Toynbee, Max Weber, and others. Cardinal John Henry Newman thought that the importance of Christianity for the Western world was to be found above all in the fact that the doctrine of Christ brought man knowledge of his nature, his dignity, and the meaning of his development. This explains the progress of the West through the centuries" (38:37).

The vision which orthodox Christianity brings to Latin America is one of yet higher peaks to scale, of far ranging scientific frontiers yet to penetrate, of universal civilization yet to attain—through energies both released and governed by the power of the Word!

Does this sound like fantasy?

Why should it?

Who but orthodox adventurers, empowered by the Word, changed the medieval world into the modern world, replaced tyrants with democracy, focused energy upon progress and so diffused the distribution of goods in the West that mankind can take to dreaming of universal prosperity?

Has not Marxism, by contrast, turned back the clock of history by restoring tyrants to absolute political power? Does not Marxism smother progress under a pall of bureaucracy, and reduce the flow of the consumer fruits of technology? Why else is such traffic as goes over the Berlin Wall all in one Westward direction?

The very core of orthodoxy across the history of the Church lies in the implicit or explicit recognition that *energy* is of the earth, earthy, while *power* is from God—dispensed via His Word.

The fulcrum to which orthodox Christianity turns to move the world is the Word of God, as revealed in the Scriptures, and courageously preached from multiplying pulpits!

20

Four Facets of Orthodoxy

We have previously discussed the four pillars of Marxism and discovered these also in the structure of Liberation Theology.

It is possible to discern four factors at work in the social impact of orthodoxy. Briefly:

a) The power: supplied by God, the active presence of the Holy Spirit obedient to and implicit in the Word.

b) The vehicle: the Word as proclaimed and applied through the sermon, amplified through other teaching instruments of the Church.

c) The agent: the believer, motivated to behavior inspired and governed by the Word, an obedient praxis rooted in a renewed self and objectified in social reformation and progress.

d) The result: a body of social teaching framed in the papal Encyclicals and Protestant history. In practice, a collocation of obligation and circumstance which becomes a social program—with political, economic, and other social elements—adapted to God's will in the situation.

As pointed out above, the Word of God runs ahead of every situation, while the words of ideology are quickly outdated by events. This is why the Word is given for proclamation—a living application of divine power to living situations. A study of colonial pulpits, for example, in pre-revolutionary America, or of Puritan pulpits in pre-Cromwellian England, will indicate the intensely practical application of the dynamic Word to the changing times. The Word molded society because the preachers knew the Bible essentially by heart and were involved in their world often at the risk of their lives.

What is distinctively orthodox about the four factors just listed is the order in which they appear wherever genuinely applied.

Always the priority is with the Word. There, for orthodoxy, is the initiative, the power, the delicate adjustment to the moment beyond the present, the infinitely flexible adaptability to what God sees coming.

The orthodox believer, as we have already observed, does not permit himself to come to the Word with a program in his head, seeking texts on which to hang and justify it. This is ideology.

Orthodoxy, unlike LT, makes no attempt to "use" the Bible for purposes determined by "theological reflection" drawn from other sources. Orthodoxy seeks to *under*-stand the Word by *standing*-under it in the posture of humble obedience. The believer does not use the truth; he implores the "truth" to use him!

We think, as one of many examples, of Calvin's Geneva where the four factors noted above can be readily discerned.

The Word preached proclaimed God's concern with the plight of the poor. But begging, which was endemic throughout Europe, appears in the Scriptures only in a derogatory light. At best, as between poor Lazarus and rich Dives (Luke 16:20-25), the beggar puts love to the test. So in social response to the Word Geneva forbade begging.

What then? Starvation? The welfare state?

No, neither.

Starvation among children all descended from the same original parents? Clearly forbidden by the Scriptures: "But if any one who has the world's goods and sees his brother in need, yet closes his heart against him, how does God's love abide in him" (I John 3:17)?

As to a welfare system which makes work optional, the Bible clearly teaches that God-given talents are for use—man is to work to provide for himself and the needy: "If any will not work, let him not eat" (II. Thess. 3:10); and, "Let the thief no longer steal, but rather let him labor, doing honest work with his hands, so that he may be able to give to those in need" (Eph. 4:28).

So Geneva, in obedient response to the Word preached, establishes a variety of work-study, work-apprentice, even state-financed work programs, enough so that observers like German sociologist Ernst Troeltsch speak of Genevan "Christian Socialism."

What we are stressing here is that *in response* to the Word preached, a community develops programs to heed the Word's mandates, and does so by the Word's power and within the Word's moral parameters.

"This Socialism is thoroughly anti-Communist," says German scholar Ernst Troeltsch in his scholarly *Social Teaching of the Christian Churches*, "but everywhere it makes the community responsible for the individual members, and in certain instances requires the greatest sacrifices of public and private means. In all this the clergy were the driving force" (85:II,903).

Here, as always in the impact of Christian orthodoxy, there are the four factors mutually at work: the demands of the Word preached, the power the Word exudes to pursue obedience to its demands, the believing community and the development of practical programs to incarnate communal obedience.

Was this, then, but an isolated and exceptional example of orthodoxy's molding society?

Quite to the contrary, Geneva was but typical of the fermentation introduced into human culture by the Word of God proclaimed by the Church.

What is indispensable, if the example of Geneva is to be understood and its incalculable influence upon Western history is to be assessed, is the discovery that preacher John Calvin did not arrive at the city he was to immortalize with a sheaf of ideological social blueprints under his arm.

Intending only to pass through Geneva, in the summer of 1536, en route to scholarly pursuits elsewhere, Calvin was obliged through the imprecations hurled upon his "timidity" by the city's lone Reformer, William Farel, to join Farel as preacher of the Word. More than preacher Calvin never wished to be; citizen (bourgeois) of the city he did not even become until 1559.

All he had, and all that accounts for his immense influence upon Western history, was the *power* of the Word: 1) *preached* from his pulpit in Geneva's San Pierre, and 2) *practised* under the vigilent eye of that unique ecclesiastical creation, which Protestantism substituted for the Catholic confessional, the "Consistoire de Geneve!" (46).

And it worked!

Geneva became an example of the Word powerfuly at work at the heart of a society, an example preceded by many communions before Calvin's time and followed by many thereafter.

And John Calvin would but join a long lineage of believers in the power of God's Word in saying to us now something like: Are you really surprised, O you of little faith, that the *Word of God* which created all things, and man too, can also recreate us in God's own image, and transform our social habitation into a disciplined *communion,* that is, a community knit by the bonds of love?

Those who can, in fact, marvel at the power resident in Holy Bibles preached in countless tongues will rejoice that the Word which made and sustains heaven and earth can, where believed, make man and his communities "new!"

21

The Bible and the Church

We turn now to delineate more precisely how the power of the Word, channeled through the Church, fashioned the enormous strides taken by the West, and offers the same to the "Third World."

For preaching was the Church established; to this end the Church is ever called: "Preach the word, be urgent in season and out of season, convince, rebuke, and exhort . . ." (II Tim. 4:2). So Paul commands his spiritual son Timothy, typical of the line of pulpiteers from his day to this!

The pulpit transcends the ideologue; the sermon banishes ideology.

How, precisely?

Let us turn once more to Calvin, under whose influence several generations of pulpiteers called democratic revolutions into being:

"Here, then, is the sovereign power with which the pastors of the church, by whatever name they be called, ought to be endowed. That they may dare boldly to do all things by God's Word; may compel all worldly power, glory, wisdom, and exaltation to yield to and obey his majesty; supported by his power, may command all from the highest even to the last; may build up Christ's household and cast down Satan's; may feed the sheep and drive away the wolves; may instruct and exhort the teachable; may accuse, rebuke, and subdue the rebellious and stubborn; may bind and loose; finally, if need be, may launch thunderbolts and lightnings; but do all things by God's Word" (16:IV.8.9).

Observe how all begins and ends with "by God's Word." The pulpit comes with but one conception of transforming power: "All things by God's Word!" The Church has its authority only as channel for power from the Word to which it gives, and demands, obedience. This is orthodoxy!

A century after Calvin practised his own instruction and thus made Geneva into what refugee visitor John Knox called "the veriest school of Christ," one of Calvin's successors in England, Thomas Case, challenged thus the British House of Commons, then under the leadership of Puritan Oliver Cromwell: "Reformation must be universal! Reform all places, all persons and all callings; reform the benches of parliament, the inferior magistrates. Reform the universities, reform the cities, reform the counties, reform inferior schools of learning, reform the Sabbath, reform the ordinances, the worship of God. . . . You have more work to do than I can speak!" (90:10-11).

The Church in the West fulfilled its divine mandate.

The Word was gotten out.

And what is now called "the Western world" took its place in history.

22

Word and Revolution

Has the Word of God inspired revolution, as the words of Marx have bred rebellion?

Does, then, the Word of God hold out hope, now, to the oppressed of Latin America, a hope as genuine as that of Marxism/LT is spurious?

Does history in fact show that Christian orthodoxy has been the dynamic source of social progress?

We have already listened to Karl Jaspers and others who say so.

Has Christian orthodoxy, then, actually fomented liberating revolutions?

Exactly so!

We turn here to one stream of orthodoxy, that flowing out the Geneva of John Calvin. Not because we count it the only example of the power of the Word in the West, but because it most aptly beckons those most concerned with spreading democracy and its fruits in Latin America and elsewhere.

Christianity has overthrown tyrannies, both political and economic!

Let us take note of that, with an eye on those presently duped by ideology, and misled into thinking that "liberation" resides in the words of Marx/Liberation Theology!

We turn to Calvinism, then, only as illustrative of the immense power available to all those who today hunger and thirst after righteousness.

"The most characteristic and influential form of Protestantism in the two centuries following the Reformation," writes R.H. Tawney in his *Religion and the Rise of Capitalism,* "is that which descends, by one path or another, from the teaching of Calvin. Unlike the Lutheranism from which it sprang, Calvinism, assuming different shapes in different countries, became an international movement, which brought, not peace but a sword, and the path of which was strewn with revolutions."

Calvinism, *the epitome of Christian orthodoxy,* leaves a path through history which was "strewn with revolutions!?"

Precisely!

And who is R. H. Tawney to say so?

Tawney, member of the British Labor Party, advisor to the British Embassy in Washington, was Professor of Economic History at the University of London through World War II. The book from which this quotation is taken has long been recognized a classic in its field—written in a style, incidentally, which adds zest to economic history!

But Tawney is not alone. Marxist Leon Trotsky somewhere observes that the two most radical political forces loosed into Western history since the Reformation rise respectively from Marx and . . . Calvin! Trotsky perceived in Calvin/Calvinism what most school textbooks ignore, and thus it comes as a surprise, perhaps, to our readers that the clearest voice for Christian orthodoxy issued, in the view of one of the ablest Marxists of our century, a call for revolution!

"Calvinism was," Tawney continues, "an active and radical force. It was a creed which sought, not merely to purify the individual, but to reconstruct Church and State, and to renew society by penetrating every department of life, public as well as private, with the influence of religion" (83:91).

Herbert D. Foster, professor of history at Dartmouth College early in this century, traces the following revolutions to Calvinist orthodoxy: in Geneva, 1536; in Scotland, 1559, 1567; in the Dutch Declaration of Independence, 1581; the Huguenot civil wars in France, culminating in the Edict of Nantes, 1598; Bocskay's Hungerian revolt of 1606; the Scottish Covenanters, 1638; the English Civil War of the 1640s and Revolution of 1688; the American revolution of 1776 (34:148,160).

Few have, along with Tawney, caught the revolutionary implications of Calvinism more acutely than Michael Walzer, professor of politics at Princeton. *The Revolution of the Saints* is Walzer's title for a study of orthodoxy and the English Revolution of the 1640s, and he subtitles his lively book, "A Study in the Origins of Radical Politics"—the politics of the orthodox!

"The Calvinist saint," Walzer says, "is above all, an extraordinarily bold, inventive, and ruthless politician, as a man should be who has 'great works' to perform, as a man, perhaps, must be for 'great works have great enemies' " (90:vii). He is quoting "great works to perform" from Puritan pastor Stephen Marshall, preached as revolution got under way in 1641.

The seed of the Word, spread by the lips of orthodoxy, sprang up in democratic revolutions.

But why?

Let us move thoughtfully here. The eyes of countless "saints" who risked or gave their lives that we might enjoy freedom are perchance upon us.

Why should the Bible, God's inspired Word, dutifully preached evoke revolution? Who, listening to typically tepid sermonizing today, would ever think so?

Well, no one thought so, necessarily. Puritans simply found it happening!

Still, then, why?

The answer suggested by some observation of Word-empowered revolutions at last becomes almost obvious. It is this:

The Word of God resists restraint. This makes the pulpit which intends to proclaim that Word also restless with restraint. The Word shatters shackles! "Truth" faithfully preached liberates first the proclaimer and then the proclaimed-to because the Word itself reaches for freedom and creates it!

In his Genevan pulpit Calvin was a channel to the power that frees, and he fought for absolute non-interference from both political and economic forces. The free pulpit requires the free society. Puritans fought for political liberty for only one reason: that the Word, and obedience to it, might be unimpeded by any tyranical hand. Bowing humbly before God, to recall Macaulay's apt metaphor, *required* setting a foot upon the neck of autocracy!

If the West did not take its liberties for granted, this would be obvious! A glance at the totalitarian states, and the strictures imposed upon pulpits there, clarifies precisely the role which the pulpit came to play in the struggles which won democracy for the West. Demanding freedom for proclamation of the Word, the pulpit forged freedom for its world.

What orthodox Christianity brought democracy to one land after another to ensure was, quite simply, freedom for "straight speech!" Unable to live with tyranny, the Church fought by word and with sword for liberty. The power of the Word came to shape the form taken by the politics, and political liberty came to characterize the West! As simple, and as bloody, as that!

The Puritans who most actively embodied orthodoxy demanded a political structure that guaranteed what they called "Freedom Of Worship"—meaning the unhampered right (indeed, the politically protected right, as embodied in the First Amendment, finally, to the American Constitution) to hear, and to do, the Word of the Lord.

Freedom of religion turned out to be incompatible with political tyranny.

It began in Geneva and spread across Western Europe and the Atlantic.

And while it is true, as their detractors are quick to point out, that the Puritans intended to control through the Church the political liberties they won, in fact freedom of the pulpit inevitably proved to be contagious.

And the point must be emphasized: just as the words of ideology lead to a totalitarianism which stifles all facets of life, so the Word of God leads to a democracy which liberates all facets of life.

And so it was, that despite Puritan reluctance, the democratic state which orthodoxy created could not but spread freedom around—could not always, indeed, prevent the degeneration of liberty into license, the mortal danger which, as Aristotle long ago observed, always threatens a free people—and gravely endangers the West today.

Puritan-won democracy almost at once came to provide liberty for free enterprise. Calvinism's influence upon the rise of capitalism, first stressed by German sociologist Max Weber in his now famous *The Protestant Ethic and the Spirit of Capitalism* (92), has become the substance of a large body of learned discussion—the thrust of which is that liberty for the pulpit implied, and soon became, liberty for the entrepeneur.

With political democracy, too, came the rise of free inquiry which hosted the Renaissance development of science, both theoretical and applied, so characteristic of the West. Free education followed, and this was stimulated by orthodox Christians intent upon a citizenry capable of serving God at their best: not only to work, but to work well!

In sum, at the root of Western progress is democracy; at the root of Western democracy is Christian orthodoxy.

All because, we repeat, orthodox revolutionaries sought, and overthrew tyrannies to ensure, a state which made room for the free and untrammeled pulpit and free and untrammeled life of obedience to it.

And they were, as Hannah Arendt carefully observed, *revolutionaries* and not rebels! The orthodox had no truck with negation, nor the negation of the negation, hoping for the better. Christians overturned one form of government in the light of another already formulated in their minds. Formulated, that is, to ensure the free pulpit and clear conscience. The rest would wait upon the Word!

Thanks to orthodoxy the West enjoys freedom with all its potential—and all its risks!

As the word of Marx makes rebels, so the Word of the Lord creates revolutionaries!

"The Calvinist Church was an army marching back to Canaan," Tawney says, "under orders delivered once for all from Sinai, and the aim of its leaders was the conquest of the Promised Land, not the consolation of stragglers or the encouragement of laggards" (83:115).

Yes, the "Revolution of the Saints"—Professor Walzer is right about that!

Sir Ernest Barker, Cambridge University Professor of Politics, writes, "I am inclined to believe that Book IV, chapter 20, section 31 of the *Institutes* [of Calvin] is one of the seed-beds of modern liberty. It passed into the Huguenot writings of the years 1572-9 . . . and through them into the Dutch Declaration of Independence, or Act of Abjuration, of 1581. . . . Through them again it passed, by ways I shall endeavor to trace, into the English Revolution and Bill of Rights of the year 1689. . . . In New England as well as in Old England Puritanism was thus a force which helped lay the foundations of a free Commonwealth, freely based on the common purposes and consent of its members" (6:126).

Historian Will Durant, retracing the ground we have already surveyed through the eyes of Barker and Foster, puts the Calvinist story in his own way:

"The stoicism of a hard creed made strong souls of Scottish Covenanters, the English and Dutch Puritans, the Pilgrims of New England. . . . It encouraged brave and ruthless men to win a continent and spread the base of education and self-government until all men could be free."

And then Durant summarizes the inevitable evolution we have been talking about: "Men who chose their own pastors soon claimed the right to choose their own governors, and the self-ruled congregation became the self-governed municipality" (28:489).

To ask how we got where we are in the West, on mankind's long pilgrimage through time, is to hear Cromwell's Roundheads chanting Genevan psalms as they marched to battle against King Charles I, to hear John Knox confronting Queens Mary and Elizabeth who threatened his life as he demanded liberty for his Scottish pulpit, to see Pilgrims kneeling, like the Pope of today, to kiss the good earth they died to make the seat of a free state.

Writing in his classic *Social Contract,* an ideological treatise which played its role in fostering rebellion in France in 1789, Jean Jacques Rousseau has this footnote concerning the Calvin into whose Geneva, half a century after Calvin's death, he was born:

"Those who know Calvin only as a theologian much under-estimate the extent of his genius. . . . Whatever changes time may bring in our religion, so long as the spirit of patriotism and liberty still lives among us, the memory of this great man will be forever blessed" (76:401).

Rousseau might be surprised to read the obloquies commonly heaped upon "this great man" by those who abuse the freedom of speech he fought to obtain for them. For this is what Calvin himself had to say about political democracy:

"Magistrates ought to apply themselves with the highest diligence to prevent the freedom, whose guardians they have been appointed, from being in any respect diminished, far less violated," Calvin writes in his *Institutes*. "If they are not sufficiently alert and careful, they are faithless in office, and traitors to their country" (16:IV.20.8).

And how, then, should "traitors" to liberty be dispossessed of their tyrannical authority? Calvin answers in the words which Sir Ernest Barker refers to as "one of the seedbeds of modern liberty."

Citizens, Calvin says, have no right to rebellion. But they have, under express circumstances, the duty of revolution. Recalling the "ephors" in ancient Sparta, and the "tribunes" in Rome, both appointed to protect the rights of the people, Calvin calls upon minor office-holders to lead revolt against "kings who violently fall upon and assault the lowly common folk." It was a stipulation upon which Calvin insisted when, during his lifetime, efforts were made in his native France to secure Protestant liberties by a rising against the King in France (46).

And what, then, if the lesser magistrate fails to mount a revolution against the tyrant? "I declare their dissimulation involves nefarious perfidy, because they betray the freedom of the people" (16:IV.20.31).

The call of orthodoxy for revolution!

How disciplined as compared with a rebellion fueled by hate and destined to replace bad tyranny with worse!

Over several centuries, ranging from the 1560s into the 1900s, Christian orthodoxy established a kind of political ratio: the free pulpit required the free society; the free society profits most from its liberties if it takes the the meaning of its freedom from the Word which the pulpit enunciates in "straight speech!"

In brief,

IF one minimizes, or fails to comprehend, the dynamics of history as Christian orthodoxy perceives them, THEN the notion that revolutions were mounted 'merely' for the freedom to preach and obey the Bible may seem an egregious misconception.

BUT IF one grasps the orthodox conviction that transforming *power* waits in the wings of history upon infusion through the Word, THEN the notion that revolutions were mounted to provide that Word with pulpits free to call that Word to the stage of time becomes transparently sober political analysis, an exciting reading of Western history and concrete hope for a better day among the exploited of the earth.

This Word, forthrightly preached, has the power to make "new" both the exploiter and the exploited, both the rich and the poor, both the believer and the ideologue—and to reform the structure of the society they together sustain.

But where is this Word forthrightly and courageously preached today?

This is the challenge which faces a genuinely "liberating" theology!

We conclude with pointing to a model of what orthodox preaching has done in the Western world, a model for what can be done through the same power in Latin America and elsewhere!

23

Orthodoxy and the American Revolution

Latin America can take heart from "reflection" upon the revolution which orthodoxy in the form of Puritanism, its roots deep in Calvinism, mounted in the colonial United States. Given the same reliance upon the power of the Word of God, what happened in North America can happen to the South!

Orthodoxy called a free nation into existence. This is the testimony of a steadily growing number of competent witnesses, coming forward after a period (still enshrined in school textbooks) which found itself incapable of understanding or appreciating America's orthodox religious foundations.

Twice-honored with the Pulitzer Prize for Literature, distinguished American historian Samuel Eliot Morison writes in his monumental *Oxford History of the American People,* "In the broadest sense Puritanism was a passion for righteousness; the desire to know and do God's will. . . . Puritan ways of thinking and doing have had a vast effect on the American mind and character, precursors of what is commonly called the Protestant Ethic" (70:61).

"Much that the Puritans wrote has been deservedly forgotten, but the dust has gathered as well upon the works of some who, when brought into the light of the present, appear to have been powerful instruments in working out the social and political, as well as the religious and cultural, destiny of America." So say Professors Perry Miller and Thomas H. Johnson of Harvard in the Preface to their collection of American Puritan sermons and documents, titled *The Puritans* (65:v).

Writing in 1956, Professor Miller describes his personal absorption in pursuit of the influence of Puritans and Puritanism upon the origins and development of American culture and institutions: "To the elucidation of this story I, in common with several historians of my generation, have devoted my life; to this investigation, I dedicate what remains of it" (62:vii).

The fruits of this singular devotion appeared first in *Orthodoxy in Massachusetts, 1630-1650* to be followed by a large number of publications, the most impressive being Professor Miller's *The New England Mind* in two substantial volumes. The obligation to Puritanism which he assumed at a time when "scholarship" all but ignored its history, Miller adds, became "the mission of expounding what I took to be the innermost propulsion of the United States" (62:viii).

"I am convinced," he says, "that in expounding the federal marrow of Puritan theology I am calling attention to a constellation of ideas basic to any comprehension of the American mind . . . an essential continuity between the New England theology and that of the Reformed, or as they are called, the Calvinist churches [because] . . . in historical perspective, their way of interpreting the Bible must be called Calvinist" (62:49).

In the first volume of his *New England Mind,* Miller puts it this way: "Regardless of the repute in which it may be held today, Puritanism is of immense historical importance; it was not only the most coherent and most powerful single factor in the early history of America, it was a vital expression of a crucial period in European development, and those who would understand the modern world must know something of what it was and of what heritages it has bequeathed to the present" (63:I,viii).

Harvard University philosopher Ralph Barton Perry devotes an entire volume to *Puritanism and Democracy*.

"I claim only," he writes, "that a large part of the distinctively American tradition, culture, institutions, and nationality consists in two systems of ideals: the puritanism implanted in the seventeenth century, and the democratic creed disseminated in the eighteenth century. . . . the puritan philosophy has formed an important part of that fundamental agreement of mind and purpose by which the United States has played its peculiar role in the modern world" (73:34).

Further on in his study, Perry concludes: "It is safe to assume, then, that the influence of puritanism, in the broad Calvinistic sense, was a major force in the late colonial period, and that it contributed uniquely and profoundly to the making of the American mind when the American mind was in the making" (73:81).

But was Puritanism at odds with the spirit of democracy, as is so commonly supposed?

"It is not necessary, therefore," Professor Perry answers, "that the later historian should build a bridge from puritanism to democracy. The puritans themselves built such a bridge, and many of them crossed it, some decades before John Locke. Men such as Cromwell, Milton, Williams and Penn belong to the history of protestantism and the history of democracy" (73:358-59).

Quoting A.S.P. Woodhouse's *Puritanism and Liberty,* Perry says, "As Professor Woodhouse summarizes the matter, puritanism 'evolved from its theological consciousness ideas of liberty, of equality, of individualism, of government by consent and agreement, and of a species of privilege which had nothing to do with worldly possessions or existing class distinctions' " (73:358).

Referring to what he calls "the profound democratic implications inherent in the fundamental ideas of puritanism," Perry adds, "it was a short and natural step from the view that 'in the order of grace all believers are equal' to the view that 'in the order of nature all men are equal' " (73:357, 358).

In a word, "It has been forgotten that Calvin himself through his insistence on the superiority of the spiritual to the temporal power was a political revolutionary, in theory as well as in act. . . . Through the habit of identifying Calvinism with its excesses posterity has lost sight of the close and continuous association between Calvinism and the ideas that constitute the basic creed of democracy. . . . The most significant symbol of this kinship is Locke himself. For if John Locke was the father of modern democracy, he was nonetheless a descendent of Calvin. 'Through direct and indirect influences, both orthodox and liberal, Locke became,' as a recent writer has expressed it, "a carrier" of Calvinism from the Reformation to the revolutions of 1688 and 1776' " (73:197). Professor Perry is quoting Herbert Foster whose attribution of ten revolutions to the influence of Calvin we have noted earlier.

Yale Professor Sydney E. Ahlstrom writes in his massive *Religious History of the American People,* "Indeed, Puritanism provided the moral and religious background of fully 75 percent of the people who declared their independence in 1776" (1:124). Ahlstrom declares, "The *Federalist Papers,* published in 1787-88, as well as John Adams's defenses of the American constitutions, can be read as Puritan contributions to Enlightenment political theory" (1:363).

Of "the Reformed tradition," Ahlstrom observes earlier in his study, "the total outlook involved in this rigorous and radical conception of Christianity implied a whole new social order. . . . the expansion of Reformed and Puritan convictions had revolutionary implications; it was a threat to arbitrary and despotic government" (1:116).

"Elemental to this transforming power," Ahlstrom says, "was the knowledge that God rules the world which he made, that the earth is the Lord's, that all the orders and stations thereof are good, and that man's highest worldly duty is to glorify God. Sloth and idleness dishonor the Creator" (1:117).

As to roots of Puritanism: "In fact, Holy Scripture was both the practical and theoretical fountainhead of the movement. . . . Puritanism was a 'movement of the Book' among an increasingly literate people . . ." (1:92).

The reader will observe that Professor Ahlstrom essentially summarizes the thesis of this section of our study: an orthodoxy which roots in the Bible becomes the fountainhead of revolutions, among them the revolution which established the United States of America.

And how was the power of the Bible infused into the Puritan mind and community: "On the Sabbath there were morning and afternoon services—each with its lengthy free prayers, discordantly sung psalms, and a very long sermon. The sermons, delivered in plain style on a wide range of subjects, offered solid biblical exposition, stated the doctrine explicitly, and gave particular attention to its practical 'use' " (1:148). Ahlstrom is describing the Massachusetts Bay towns, but it was a pattern repeated throughout New England.

And through the sermonizing flowed the power which achieved what Marx and Liberation Theology seek vainly to focus energy upon: the making of the "new man." "Of all the achievements of Puritanism, however, none was more important than that which the Puritan himself would have insisted to be a work of God: its capacity to shape a type of person. . . . And it is no small feat that the colony itself would shape a new generation of men and women—even a long posterity" (1:150).

It is no coincidence that a student of Calvinism holds that for Calvin himself the highest work of art known to man was a "new" self sculpted by the power of the Word after the lineaments of the divine Image recreated through faith (93).

"The sermon," says Michael Walzer, "was transformed into a manual of spiritual technology," and "the saint's personality was his own most radical innovation" (90:145;3).

Let us conclude by listening to Puritan Cotton Mather, whose ancestry played its role in establishing the New England mind which, as we have been pointing out, "flowered" into the American Revolution.

Looking back, in the 1790s, to the founding of New England, Mather pens his massive *Magnalia Christi Americana*—a magnificent two-volume account of the "Great Works of Christ in America" as these are reflected in the founding and expansion of the Puritan commonwealth on the shores of New England.

The Pilgrims, Mather says, "sold their estates to put the money into a common stock for the welfare of the whole." Having done so, they embarked in faith, their "proposal" being: "We ask a shrine for faith and simple prayer, Freedom's sweet waters and untainted air."

Having been delayed in departure from Europe, they did not sight the new world until late November. Upon landing on the wintry coast, "The hardships they encountered were attended with, and productive of, deadly sicknesses, which in two or three months carried off more than half their company. . . . What a wonder it was that all the bloody savages far and near did not cut off this little remnant . . . but this people of God were come to a wilderness to worship Him; and so He kept their enemies from such attempts as would otherwise have annihilated this poor handful of men, thus far already diminished" (60:52, 54).

The orthodox accepted in faith all the risks which their pursuit of "freedom of worship" imposed. They survived the winter, survived hostile attack, survived temptation to depart the Way, the Truth and the Life set before them by the Word—and set America on a course destined to make of her a model of liberty and progress.

And while in due season Puritan orthodoxy lent its leading ideas to the American Declaration of Independence and ensuing revolution, French ideology composed a Declaration of the Rights of Man and mounted a rebellion destined to end in tyranny.

24

Renewal of Orthodoxy

Why has Christian orthodoxy grown so disengaged that few even suspect its revolutionary history? Why is it, indeed, so easily equated with reaction, while Marxism appears as so much more progressive?

Cotton Mather anticipated that, in a way, and tried in his *Magnalia* to warn orthodoxy as Tolstoy and Dostevsky tried to warn Russia.

The colonies which Puritans had so willingly died to found were, Mather already observed, loosening their ties with the Word of God powerfully preached. And though, Mather says, "One would expect that as the colonists grew in their estates, they would grow in their payment of their quit-rents unto the God who gives them power to get wealth, by more liberally supporting His ministers and ordinances among them, the most likely way to save them from most miserable apostasy," yet he fears that the colonials are already likely to bear out the ancient adage,

"Religion brought forth prosperity, and the daughter destroyed the mother" (60:63).

Prosperity was given America; the bounteous power of God has never ceased impelling the hands that wrest riches of all kinds from earth, air, water and the human spirit.

But such prosperity has indeed dulled the ear in the pew, diminished the ardor of the pulpit and turned many from the Word altogether, exactly as Mather feared.

That, in consequence, some who have a social conscience turn to alien ideologies for challenge to change is, alas, almost inevitable.

It is, moreover, two centuries since orthodoxy mounted a revolution.

Those two centuries have seen the Bible deposed in theological seminaries and university departments of religion from its orthodox status as the inspired Word of God to be viewed as a miscellaneous collection of religious documents ignored, as we have observed, at will. The "endless speculations" against which St. Paul so eloquently warns in both of his letters to Timothy have blocked the channel which God created to infuse His power into human history.

The West survives upon a heritage of orthodoxy which it widely disavows in theory and widely ignores in practice.

Meanwhile, the Lie embodied in Communist and Fascist ideologies has viciously misled and brutally abused countless millions.

Currently rebellion clothes itself with Liberationist slogans. Freedom is degraded into license.

But, alas, the counter-voice of the Church has been widely deprived of its biblical authenticity by theological speculation and ideology!

His civilization being divorced at the root from the creative Word which evoked it, Western man all too readily looks for social transformation to ideologies which in practice demonstrate their own delusions.

Oswald Spengler predicted in *The Decline of the West* (80) that Western civilization is destined to be but another of the many cultures which have risen, flourished and declined across the ages.

But so it need not be if the "Word" which orthodoxy is called to preach is poured forthrightly into the West, the Third World and those nations enslaved by ideology. This is the awesome challenge facing those who want to give their lives to re-*new*ing man and his world!

The future, not only of the West, but of all mankind rests upon the success with which this proclamation is accomplished!

What, really, could be a more revolutionary commitment than one that Christians make, perhaps all too casually, every day:

"Thy kingdom come, Thy will be done, *on earth* as it is in heaven" (Matt. 6:10)!

25

Who Cares About the Poor?

Our answer to the question, "Who cares for the poor?" is this: whoever brings the right words to their situation!

As we have seen, words engender action. Action embodies words. The words of ideology incarnate tyranny and totalitarianism. The Word of God incarnates freedom and progress of all kinds.

Who cares, *really* cares for the poor, then, not as means to his own ends but for their own sake?

Whoever preaches the Word of God, and whoever demands and supports such preaching. In short, orthodoxy, not ideology!

The rebel mentality stresses its activism.

The orthodox mentality stresses results.

The typical rebel response to criticism is to attack the critic. And the tyical Marxist/LT reaction to critique is, "We're *doing* something; all you do is talk!"

That's an easy accusation. It accords with the slogans of "class struggle" and "liberation" as one more bait for the gullible.

For it is not, in reality, an issue of who *claims* what "doing" or which "talk" is most liberating.

It is a matter of results, of track record.

Orthodox talk, in the form of preaching the Word, has an indisputable record of flowering into democracy and progress, however major are the problems waiting on resolution. Still more, orthodox preaching is key to creation of the moral atmosphere which more and more stifles exploitation and injustice, while democracy keeps open the route to reform.

Ideological activism harvests only tyranny. It is noisy and bold until silenced by the dictatorship of the proletariat.

This is no doubt why Jesus Himself chose preaching as the means to personal and social transformation. When John the Baptist asks the Christ whether He is the promised Messiah, the Lord responds by quoting the prophet Isaiah: "Go and tell John what you hear and see:

the blind receive their sight and the lame walk, lepers are cleansed and the deaf hear, and the dead are raised up, and the poor have the good news preached to them. And blessed is he who takes no offense in me" (Matt. 11:4-6, quoting Is. 35:5-6; 61:1).

The implication, however blind to it the rebel is determined to be, is unmistakable: the hope of the poor, both temporal and eternal, lies in the Word preached. This is the Lord's own determination.

"The poor" do not have the language of rebellion preached to them, nor acts of rebellion modeled for them; nor does the Lord project daily multiplication of loaves and fishes. The hope of the poor is fixed by the Lord who loves the poor upon the preaching of His Word!

And as the centuries rolled by, the poor did get "the good news preached to them"—and the West surged far ahead of the rest of the world in extending blessings of all kinds to countless millions who would otherwise have lived and died in need.

In addition, no institution in all human history has a record of more profound concern for the poor, and of greater, sustained service to their needs everywhere than the Church. Mother Teresa with her Little Sisters of the Poor is but the latest of countless saints empowered by the Word to devote selfless lives to human need—in the sharpest contrast to the inhuman brutalities characteristic of the totalitarian states. And no Word has introduced into human behavior more freedom, more scientific and social progress, and greater creation and wider distribution of goods than the "good news" which Christ ordains His appointed ministry to proclaim, and His Church to live.

Marxism/LT masquerade a concern for the poor and oppressed which, after the debris of rebellion is cleared away, multiplies murder, intensifies slavery, and mounts a more systematic exploitation of the many by the few than mankind has not known in centuries.

Who, then, cares about the poor, not as lending energy to rebellion but as persons whose names are known to God?

It is the Christ, who suffered, died and rose again who cares for the poor. And it is the Christ who decrees that His Church shall preach the liberating Word into the jungles of oppression. Well aware that this is so, the totalitarian states muzzle Christ's pulpits and permit only a "word" which, quite unlike that which resounded from Calvin's and Puritan pulpits, peddles free leases on heavenly mansions.

Orthodoxy makes no apology for choosing powerful pulpits over ideological praxis, and thus standing with the Christ to proclaim in His name and with His power the Truth which makes men free!

Study Guide

For individual stimulation and group study, we include the following brief summary of the text and questions devised to illumine each chapter.

Summary

Definitions: Marxism and Liberation Theology share a common basic structure, based on four pillars:

1. Class struggle as source of human evil
2. Private ownership of productive means as source of class struggle
3. Cure of class struggle, and thus of evil, through rebellion destroying the private ownership system
4. Self-creation of the "new man"

Liberation Theology defines itself as "critical reflection" on revolutionary praxis, limited to those who "identify" with those engaged in active rebellion.

Ideology: Marxism and LT are both ideologies, that is systems of ideas designed to coerce others through sloganizing, foment rebellion and silence conscience.

Philosophy: Marxist ideology interprets history in terms of Hegelian categories: thesis, antithesis, synthesis; negation and negation of negation.

LT Profile: Exclusivism: our way or none

Surrenders authority of Bible, creeds, tradition and Church.

Sacrifices: LT sacrifices to its Marxist commitments ten basic Christian doctrines (see text).

Alternative: Christian orthodoxy: God's Truth in "straight speech"

The Record: Words of Marxist ideology: totalitarianism

Word of God preached: democracy and progress

Distinctions: Energy is finite and placed under man's control.

Power is God's alone, infinite and alone capable of making man "new."

Rebellion: exploits energy to overthrow and demolish.

Revolution: draws upon power to replace one sociopolitical order with clearly envisioned other.

Rebellion: Becomes totalitarian because words of man which stimulate it have limited scope and flexibility, forcing tyrant to rule by sheer will.

Word Bible: Orthodoxy preaches Word of God as revealed in the Bible.

Bible and West: The progress of the West, social and political and economic, is owing to the Bible and democracy its preaching fostered.

Church and Bible: The role of the Church is to sustain pulpits which pour the power of the Word into history.

Word and Revolt: Pursuit of political freedom for the preaching and doing of God's Word has endowed the West with political democracy, of which the American Revolution is greatest example.

Hope: Orthodoxy, not ideology, is the hope of the Third World.

Questions for Thought and Discussion

1. The Goal of Marxism

1. Why is Marx sometimes called "the last of the Hebrew prophets?"
2. What was Marx's attitude toward Christianity?
3. Draw a doctrinal parallel between Marxism and Christianity.
4. Why are Marxism and Christianity basically incompatible?
5. Which two obstacles to human progress did Marx see?
6. From whom did Marx get what assistance in removing the first obstacle?
7. What one thing do Marx and Christianity have in common?
8. How did Marx deal with the second obstacle to human progress?
9. What is your reaction to Marxism?

2. The Four Pillars of Marxism

1. How do Christianity and Marxism differ in explaining the origin of human evil?
2. Explain how Marx derives the role of all social institutions from the "relations of production."
3. Explain the labor theory of value. Do you accept it?
4. Explain the theory of surplus value. Do you accept that?
5. What is the Marxist "cure" for the root of social evil?
6. How did the "revisionists" differ from Marx?
7. Who makes the decisions after the rebellion?
8. How are these new decision-makers gotten rid of?
9. Explain the fourth pillar of Marxism. Does it work?

3. Where Can You Ask That Question?

1. Why *not* Marxism?
2. Can Marxism be used only as a tool for social analysis?
3. Analyse the following possibilities:
   a. Can Marxism coexist with political freedom?
   b. Can Marxism coexist with religious freedom?
   c. Can Marxism coexist with economic freedom?
4. Compare the defects of democracy with those of Communism.
5. What is the essence of democracy?

4. What About the Four Pillars?

1. What is your evaluation of "class struggle?"
2. What is the basis for the right of private ownership? Can it be defended on non-Christian grounds?
3. Compare private and public ownership of the means of production in terms of efficiency, economy, quality.
4. Compare the Christian "new man" with the Marxist "new man."
5. Compare Russia's "new man" with Hitler's "super-race."

5. Marxism Is an Ideology

1. Define "ideology" and give some illustrations.
2. How do ideologies find followers?
3. How does ideology relate to conscience? Illustrate.
4. Name some slogans used by various ideologies. Is "Women's Lib" one?
5. Relate Hegel's "dialectic" to Marxism.
6. Does Christianity teach progress via "negation?"
7. Name some slogans presently in use in Latin America.

6. Liberation Theology Defined

1. Can Liberation Theology be discussed as one entity?
2. How does Gustavo Gutierrez define "theology" and "reflection?"
3. How does a theology become "liberating" according to Gutierrez?
4. What is the meaning, historically, of theo-logy?
5. How does LT use the "secular sciences?"

7. Liberation Theology and Marxism

1. In which two ways does LT relate itself to Marxism?
2. Why does LT opt for Marxism?
3. How does LT perceive "class struggle" in Latin America?
4. Show that LT deliberately embraces Marxism.
5. Illustrate how the Bible is warped to baptize Marxism.

8. The Four Pillars of Liberation Theology

1. How does LT try to enlist God in the class struggle?
2. Compare LT's definition of sin with that of the Bible.
3. Evaluate the slogan "institutionalized violence."
4. How does the Bible distinguish between "sin" and "evil?"
5. Why do Marxism and LT ignore the Fall?

9. Profile of Liberation Theology

1. Compare the "exclusivity" of Christianity and of LT.
2. Compare the biblical account of the Exodus with the LT version of it.
3. Give some examples of LT self-assurance.
4. Who, according to Emilio Castro, can alone do theology?
5. What does LT really mean by "identification" with the poor?
6. How would Hugo Assmann drag theology "out of its ghetto?"

10. Liberation Theology Ab-Uses the Bible

1. What is Hugo Assmann's description of the Bible? Is it yours?
2. Comment on: "The original text has become our reality and our practise." What becomes of the "Bible" this way?
3. What is meant by "the other Bible?" How does it relate to God's Word?
4. What is meant by "rereading" the Bible? What happens then?
5. Compare LT's teaching on the Holy Spirit with that of the Bible.
6. Can you think of other claims to being led by the Spirit?

11. Christian Doctrines Sacrificed to Marxism

1. Summarize in your own words LT's exposition of each of the ten basic Christian doctrines studied in the text.
2. Compare, by also using other sources if you like, the traditional, biblical form of each of these same doctrines.

12. Authentic Liberation

1. What is the basic issue between orthodox Christianity and LT?
2. How is this issue articulated by Pope John Paul II?
3. How is orthodoxy defined? What does the Greek root mean?
4. Review the "track records" of Marxism and of Christianity.
5. What is historian van Leeuwen's understanding of the root of progress?

13. Root of Freedom

1. Trace Western freedom and progress to their origin in God's Word.
2. Why have not all religions encouraged the same progress?
3. Why is freedom so readily taken for granted in the West? Is this dangerous? Why or why not?
4. What is the fundamental distinction between tyranny and democracy?

14. Energy and Power

1. Discuss the role of energy in modern civilization.
2. What are the limitations of energy?
3. Illustrate how energy is pushed beyond the range of its competence.
4. Can the application of energy cure evil? cure sin?
5. Discuss God, orthodoxy and the role of power in history.

15. Rebellion or Revolution

1. Define and illustrate the difference between rebellion and revolution.

2. Recall and evaluate Hannah Arendt's distinction between the French and the American Revolutions.
3. Compare the results of the American and the Russian Revolutions.
4. Why does LT choose the French and Russian Revolutions as models?

16. Why Successful Rebellion Becomes Totalitarian

1. Why does ideology lead inevitably to the dictator?
2. What difference between the word of Marx and the Word of God drives rebellion into totalitarianism?
3. What is Djilas seeking to teach us in his *New Class?*

17. A Deceptive Simplicity

1. How do you perceive the Bible?
2. Can you "prove" that the Bible is the Word of God?
3. What is the key to "hearing" the Word of God?
4. Show how the struggles of history revolve around "words."
5. Does the "ordinary" reader need the "expert" to hear God's Word?

18. The Word of Truth and Power

1. Discuss what words do for you.
2. Discuss what words do among people.
3. What would life be like without the power of speech and language?
4. What does the Bible mean by "Man shall live . . . by every word that proceeds from the mouth of God"?
5. What various meanings does the Bible give to the term "word?"
6. What role did "the Word" play in creation?
7. Who is that "Word?"

19. The Bible and the West

1. What do you think Jaspers means by saying, "In fact, without the Bible we fall into nothing"?
2. Have you ever thought of the Bible in that way before? If not, why not?
3. How does Christianity "secularize" nature?

4. What advantage has it been to the Western world that Christianity did "secularize" nature?
5. How is God served through work?
6. What can the Word preached out of the Bible do for Latin America?

20. Four Facets of Orthodoxy

1. Name the four facets of orthodoxy in practice.
2. Why is the order of the facets important?
3. Can you tell God's Word in advance what it must say? Why would that be ideological?
4. But are there Christian social principles regarding justice which the Word preached can imbue with power? If so, name some.

21. The Bible and the Church

1. Why does the Lord create and sustain His Church?
2. Recall and illustrate Calvin's view of the task of the pulpit.
3. Do you know pulpiteers who follow Calvin's prescription for preaching?

22. Word and Revolution

1. Give examples of orthodoxy's overthrow of tyranny.
2. Could that be done, now, wherever preaching is possible? Is this why Communist states silence the pulpit as much as they can?
3. What is the relation of Puritanism and democracy?
4. How did the search for freedom of "worship" produce democracy?
5. What is the ratio between free pulpit and free enterprise?

23. Orthodoxy and Revolution in America

1. What was the role of orthdox Christianity in the colonizing of America?
2. What is R.B. Perry's view of the relation between Puritanism and democracy?

3. What does Professor Ahlstrom consider to be the root of Puritanism?
4. Why is orthodoxy so little credited with promoting democracy?

24. Renewal of Orthodoxy

1. Provide some historical illustration of Mather's observation that "Religion brought forth prosperity, and the daughter has devoured the mother."
2. Can that observation be applied to the USA today? If so, is there a cure for that calamity?
3. Apply St. Paul's warning against "endless speculations" to current trends in theology.

25. Who Cares about the Poor?

1. Who does?
2. Is choice of God's Word instead of Marx's a desertion of the poor?
3. Why didn't Jesus preach rebellion instead of the Gospel to the poor?
4. Is the true Gospel focused only on heaven? If so, why do Communist states severely censor the pulpit?
5. Summarize in your own words the crux of this study.

Bibliography

Note: references in the text identify the source by number from the following list, and page number in that source.

1. Ahlstrom, Sydney E. *A Religious History of the American People.* New Haven:Yale, 1972.
2. Alves, Rubem. "From Paradise to Desert: Autobiographical Musings," in Gibellini, # 39.
3. Arendt, Hannah. *On Revolution.* New York: Viking, 1963.
4. Assmann, Hugo. "The Power of Christ in History," in Gibellini, # 39.
5. Assmann, Hugo. *Theology for a Nomad Church.* Trans. by Paul Burns. Maryknoll, N.Y.: Orbis, 1976.
6. Barker, Ernest. *Church, State and Study.* London: Methuen, 1930.
7. Benne, Robert. *The Ethic of Democratic Capitalism.* Philadelphia: Fortress, 1981.
8. Bernstein, Richard J. *Praxis and Action.* Philadelphia: U. of P., 1971.
9. Bigo, Pierre. *The Church and Third World Revolution.* Trans. by Sister Jeanne Marie Lyons. Maryknoll, N.Y.: Orbis, 1977.
10. Boff, Leonardo. "Christ's Liberation Via Oppression," in Gibellini, # 39.
11. Bonhoeffer, Dietrich. *Ethics.* Trans. by Neville H. Smith. New York: Macmillan, 1964.
12. Bonino, Jos Miguez. *Doing Theology in a Revolutionary Situation.* Philadelphia: Fortress, 1975.
13. Bonino, José Miguez. "Historical Praxis and Christian Identity," in Gibellini, # 39.
14. Bunyan, John. *Pilgrim's Progress.* New York: Heritage, 1942.
15. Calvez, Jean-Yves. *Politics and Society in the Third World.* Trans. by M. J. O'Connell. Maryknoll, N.Y.: Orbis, 1973.
16. Calvin, John. *Institutes of the Christian Religion.* Trans. by Ford Lewis Battles. London: SCM, 1960.
17. Camara, Helder. *Revolution Through Peace.* Trans. by Amparo McLean. New York: Harper & Row, 1971.
18. Comblin, José. *The Church and the National Security State.* Maryknoll, N.Y.: Orbis, 1979.

19. Comblin, José. "What Sort of Service Might Theology Render?" in Gibellini, # 39.
20. Davies, J.G. *Christians, Politics and Violent Revolution.* Maryknoll, N.Y.: Orbis, 1976.
21. del Valle, Luis G. "Toward a Theological Outlook," in Gibellini, # 39.
22. Deutscher, Isaac. *The Prophet Unarmed.* (Vol. III of his Life of Trotsky.) London: Oxford, 1959.
23. Diez-Alegría, José María. *I Believe in Hope.* Trans. by Gary MacEoin. New York: Doubleday, 1974.
24. Djilas, Milovan. *The New Class.* New York: Praeger, 1957.
25. Djilas, Milovan. *The Unperfect Society.* Trans. by Dorian Cooke. New York: Harcourt, Brace & World, 1969.
26. Dostoevsky, Fyodor. *The Devils.* Trans. by David Magarshack. London: Penguin, 1953.
27. Dostoevsky, Fyodor. *Memoirs from the House of the Dead.* Trans. by Jessie Coulson. London: Oxford, 1956.
28. Durant, Will. *The Reformation* (Part VI, *The Story of Civilization.*) New York: Simon & Schuster, 1957.
29. Dussel, Enrique D. "Historical and Philosophical Presuppositions for Latin American Theology," in Gibellini, # 39.
30. Eagleson, John and Scharper, Philip, eds. *Puebla and Beyond.* Trans. by John Drury. Maryknoll, N.Y.: Orbis, 1979.
31. Engels, Frederick. *Anti-Duhring.* Moscow: Foreign Languages Publishing House, 1959.
32. Feuerbach, Ludwig. *The Essence of Christianity.* Trans. by Marian Evans. Boston: Houghton, Mifflin, 1881.
33. Fierro, Alfredo. *The Militant Gospel.* Trans. by John Drury. Maryknoll, N.Y.: Orbis, 1977.
34. Foster, Herbert D. *Collected Papers of Herbert D. Foster.* Privately Printed, 1929.
35. Galilea, Segundo. "Liberation Theology and New Tasks Facing Christians," in Gibillini, # 39.
36. Garaudy, Roger. *From Anathema to Dialogue.* Trans. by Luke O'Neill. New York: Herder, 1966.
37. Gatti, Enzo. *Rich Church—Poor Church.* Trans. by Matthew J. O'Connell. Maryknoll, N.Y.: Orbis, 1974.
38. Gheddo, Piero. *Why Is the Third World Poor?* Trans. by Kathryn Sullivan. Maryknoll, N.Y.: Orbis, 1973.
39. Gibellini, Rosino, ed. *Frontiers of Theology in Latin America.* Maryknoll, N.Y.: Orbis, 1979.
40. Gollwitzer, Helmut, *et al. Du hast mich heimgesucht bei Nacht.* Munich: Kaiser, 1954.
41. Goulet, Denis. *A New Moral Order.* Maryknoll, N.Y.: Orbis, 1974.
42. Gutierrez, Gustavo. "Liberation Praxis and Christian Faith," in Gibellini, # 39.

43. Gutierrez, Gustavo. *A Theology of Liberation.* Trans. and Edited by Sister Caridad Inda and John Eagleson. Maryknoll, N.Y.: Orbis, 1973.
44. Houtart, François and Rousseau, André. *The Church and Revolution.* Trans. by Violet Nevile. Maryknoll, N.Y.: Orbis, 1971.
45. Kedward, H.R. *Fascism in Western Europe 1900-45.* New York: NYU, 1971.
46. Kingdon, Robert M. *Geneva and the Coming of the Wars of Religion in France 1555-1563.* Geneva: Droz, 1956.
47. Kirk, J. Andrew. *Theology Encounters Revolution.* Downers Grove, IL.: IVP, 1980.
48. Knox, R.A. *Enthusiasm.* Oxford: The Clarendon Press, 1950.
49. Koestler, Arthur. *Darkness at Noon.* Trans. by Daphne Hardy. New York: Macmillan, 1941.
50. Lenin, V.I. *The State and Revolution.* Moscow: Foreign Languages Publishing House, n.d.
51. Lernoux, Penny. *The Cry of the People.* New York: Doubleday, 1981.
52. Mandelstam, Nadezhda. *Hope Abandoned.* Trans. by Max Hayward. New York: Atheneum, 1974.
53. Mandelstam, Nadezhda. *Hope Against Hope.* Trans. by Max Hayward. New York: Atheneum, 1970.
54. Marx, Karl. *Capital,* Vol. I. Trans. by Samuel Moore and Edward Aveling. Moscow: Foreign Langauges Publishing House, 1961.
55. Marx, Karl. *Economic and Philosophic Manuscripts of 1844.* Trans. by Martin Milligan. Moscow: Foreign Languages Publishing House, 1961.
56. Marx, Karl and Engels, Frederick. *Manifesto of the Communist Party.* Chicago: Kerr, 1946.
57. Marx, Karl and Engels, Frederick. *Selected Correspondence 1846-1895.* Trans. by Dona Torr. New York: International Publishers, 1942.
58. Marx, Karl and Engels, Frederick. *Selected Works.* 2 vols. Moscow: Foreign Languages Publishing House, 1958.
59. Marx, Karl. *Theories of Surplus Value* (Vol. IV, of *Capital.*) Moscow: Foreign Languages Publishing House, n.d.
60. Mather, Cotton. *The Great Works of Christ in America.* 2 vols. Edinburgh: Banner of Truth reprint, 1979 (*Magnalia Christi Americana.*)
61. McCann, Dennis. *Christian Realism and Liberation Theology.* Maryknoll, N.Y.: Orbis, 1981.
62. Miller, Perry. *Errand into the Wilderness.* New York: Harper & Row, 1964.
63. Miller, Perry. *The New England Mind.* Cambridge, Mass.: Harvard, vol. I, 1939; vol. II, 1953.
64. Miller, Perry. *Orthodoxy in Massachusetts.* New York: Harper & Row, 1970.
65. Miller, Perry and Johnson, Thomas H., eds. *The Puritans.* New York: Harper & Row, 1963.
66. Miranda, José. *Marx and the Bible.* Trans. by John Eagleson. Maryknoll, N.Y.: Orbis, 1974.
67. Moltmann, Jürgen. *The Church in the Power of the Spirit.* Trans. by Margaret Kohl. New York: Harper & Row, 1977.

68. Moltmann, Jürgen. *Religion, Revolution and the Future.* Trans. by M. Douglas Meeks. New York: Scribner's, 1969.
69. Moltmann, Jürgen. *Theology ofHope.* Trans. by James W. Leitch. New York: Harper & Row, 1967.
70. Morison, Samuel E. *The Oxford History of the American People.* New York: Oxford, 1965.
71. Muñoz, Ronaldo. "The Historical Vocation of the Church," in Gibellini, # 39.
72. Novak, Michael. *The Spirit of Democratic Capitalism.* New York: American Enterprise Institute, Simon & Schuster, 1982.
73. Perry, Ralph Barton. *Puritanism and Democracy.* New York: Vanguard, 1944.
74. Petulla, Joseph M. *Christian Political Theology: A Marxian Guide.* Maryknoll, N.Y.: Orbis, 1972.
75. Quade, Quentin L., ed. *The Pope and Revolution.* Washington: Ethics and Public Policy Center, 1982.
76. Rousseau, Jean Jacques. *The Social Contract.* Trans. by G.D.H. Cole. Chicago: U. of C., 1952 (Great Books of the Western World, vol. 38.)
77. Scannone, Juan Carlos. "Theology, Popular Culture, and Discernment," in Gibellini, # 39.
78. Segundo, Juan Luis. "Capitalism Versus Socialism: Crux Theologica," in Gibellini, # 39.
79. Serge, Victor. *Memoirs of a Revolutionary 1901-1941.* Trans. by Peter Sedgwick. London: Oxford, 1963.
80. Spengler, Oswald. *The Decline of the West.* Abridged by Helmut Werner. Trans. by Arthur Helps. New York: Knopf, 1962'
81. Steiner, George. *Tolstoy or Dostoevsky.* New York: Knopf, 1956.
82. Stumme, Wayne, ed. *Christians & the Many Faces of Marxism.* Minneapolis: Augsburg, 1984.
83. Tawney, R. H. *Religion and the Rise of Capitalism.* New York: Mentor, 1954.
84. Toynbee, Arnold J. *The Study of History.* Abridged by D.C. Somervell in 2 vols. New York: Oxford, 1947, 1957.
85. Troeltsch, Ernst. *The Social Teaching of the Christian Churches.* 2 vols. Trans. by Olive Wyon. New York: Macmillan, 1931.
86. Trotsky, Leon. *Literature and Revolution.* Ann Arbor, MI.: U. of M., 1960.
87. Ulum, Adam B. *The Bolsheviks.* New York: Macmillan, 1965.
88. Van Leeuwen, Arend Th. *Christianity in World History.* Trans. by H.H. Hoskins. New York: Scribner's, 1964.
89. Vidales, Raul. "Methodological Issues in Liberation Theology," in Gibellini, # 39.
90. Walzer, Michael. *The Revolution of the Saints.* Cambridge, Mass.: Harvard, 1965.
91. Wasiolek, Edward. *Dostoevsky, The Major Fiction.* Cambridge, Mass.: M.I.T., 1964.
92. Weber, Max. *The Protestant Ethic and the Spirit of Capitalism.* Trans. by Talcott Parsons. London: Allen & Unwin, 1930.

93. Wencelius, Leon. *L'Esthétique de Calvin.* Paris: Societe d'Edition "Les Belles Lettres," n.d.
94. Wertenbaker, Thomas J. *The Puritan Oligarchy.* New York: Grosset & Dunlap, 1947.